BACKSTAGE
PASS

Behind the Scenes Access to Rock Star Quality Recipes and how I came up with them

EDDIE LANCE

BACKSTAGE PASS

Copyright © 2019 by Eddie Lance
All rights reserved.

Thank you, Robin Lance, Ryan Lance, Jenna Lance, and Makala Neal, for inspiration.

Cover design: by Melanie Mongar
Interior Designed by Nonon Tech & Design

Printed in the United States of America.

Library of Congress Control Number:
ISBN: 978-0-578-59771-3

AUTHOR'S NOTE

The recipes in this book are a combination of ones I wrote myself, along with adaptations of recipes I've run across over the years.

In 1971, Five Man Electrical Band wrote and recorded the song Signs. Tesla covered it in 1990, making it their own and it became one of their greatest hits. I apply this same concept to my recipes. I've covered many over the years, and I encourage everyone to do the same. Even the ones you'll read about here. Make changes to your personal taste.

SETLIST

Openers

Tavern Jerky 26

Smoked Wings 60

Salsa...38

Millie's Mexican Salsa 40

Quesadilla 44

Spinach and Artichoke Dip 50

Millie's Mexican Dip..56

Southwest Eggrolls 86

Avocado Dip 88

Headliners

Smoked Brisket 75

Stuffed Baked Potatoes 79

Enchilada Lil' Suzi 95

Oven-Baked Sandwiches 100

Burnt Vegan Ends 106

Smoked Brisket Pizza.. 127

Whiskey Brisket Pizza 131

iii

Buffalo Chicken Pizza 133

Thai Chicken Pizza 135

BBQ Chicken Pizza 136

Dandy Lion Prime Rib 141

Sweet Sandwiches 149

All in the pool pasta 150

Encores

Fried Ice Cream 30

Divinity 89

Kolache 113

Mom's Apple Pie 145

Road Crew

Sproke 11

Hamburger Seasoning 17

Asian Slaw 34

Blues Vegan BBQ Sauce 108

ED Rub BBQ Seasoning 65

Captain Jack Whiskey Sauce 132

Buffalo Sauce 134

FOREWARD

by Brian Wheat

Let me tell you about my friend Eddie Lance. I met Eddie when he was young. He was a Tesla fan and he had started a campaign to get Tesla back together after we had broken up in the mid 90's called Operation Reunite Tesla.

I had started another band at this time called Soulmotor. Eddie swears to this day he sent me a $10 cash (which I never received) for one of our CD's, so there's been an ongoing joke about it over the years but me and Eddie have developed a very good friendship and have become quite good friends.

Eddie and I often get barbecue at Gates BBQ when I play Tesla shows in Kansas City. He must really enjoy it because a few years ago, he started telling me that he had begun barbecuing and was making wood fired BBQ pizzas and other smoked meats such as brisket and pork. When I found out I would be playing a show in Omaha where Eddie lives on a Def Leppard tour, I called him and asked him if he could try to make me some vegan barbecue and burnt ends. He took the challenge and it was amazing.

This book here is a tribute to Eddie's barbecue pit master specialties and everything else he makes. All the best Eddie! Don't get no barbecue sauce on your chin!

LOST TREASURE

The Omaha Stockyards were founded in 1883 by a group of investors. The Stockyards provided hundreds of jobs at the yards themselves and the meat packing factories that popped up nearby. Before refrigeration was invented, the only way to keep meat fresh was to keep the animals alive for as long as possible. Meat packing plants only bought animals when they were needed. The Stockyards charged a simple fee to the ranchers and served as a holding spot for their animals until they were sold. This meant that large groups of livestock would often been seen huddling together across the yards for everyone to see. This was a practice that was still in use when a certain Nebraskan came to town.

In 1885, a young man from Omaha was working at the Stockyards in one of the meat processing plants. He worked, day in and day out, handling slabs of meat in the dull little factory he was constantly cooped up in. He had dreamed of a better life for a very long time, and one day, he decided it was time to make his move. He got word that there was a shipment of gold worth $60,000 that was to be shipped to a bank in Lincoln, NE. He decided to rob the train that would be carrying the gold after overhearing a conversation about the shipment. From this conversation, he learned that the train would be leaving the next morning from a station located 50 miles southwest of Lincoln.

As the train grew closer to Lincoln, the engineer was exasperated when he suddenly noticed a sizeable herd of cattle blocking the tracks. He immediately slowed down the train and blew a warning blast of the whistle in hopes to scare off the cattle. The conductor breathed a sigh of relief when it seemed to have worked, but just as he was about to speed up again the young man from Omaha appeared right next to him with a gun in his hand. He calmly but firmly ordered the conductor to stop the train. He managed to get away with all the gold without a hitch, leaving the engineer unconscious, but not seriously injured, by knocking him in the head with his gun.

The bandit loaded the heavy bags of gold onto a wagon and took off on a horse that carried him and his loot towards Central City where he had planned to relocate and start the new life he dreamed of. As it turned out, he had not planned everything out as well as he'd hoped. The weight of the gold he had heaped into the wagon made the contraption difficult to pull for the single horse who also had to carry the man himself. After crossing the Big Blue River near what is now Staplehurst, the horse had to slow down until he was only managing a brisk walk. Not long after that, the horse had stopped completely. The man found himself in need of a new horse, so while he went out searching, he decided to bury the stolen gold in the prairie, covering it up with underbrush so that it was not noticeable. He abandoned the wagon and the tired old horse to search for a replacement that would carry him to the life of his dreams.

Unknown to the man, a pack of deputies were already hot on his trail. Not long after the deputies had set out, they began to catch up with their target and found the wagon and horse where he had abandoned them. Thinking that he may have hid the gold somewhere nearby, they split up into two groups to search the surrounding terrain. One group began searching for the stolen gold between the hidden transportation and where the train had stopped, and the other group resumed looking for the bandit.

The next day, a farmer woke with the rising sun, only to find the thief in his barn trying to steal one of his horses. He took his trusty shotgun off the wall and shot the thief. The young man had tried desperately to explain what had happened in the past 24 hours and why he needed the horse, but the farmer could not understand all of what he was saying. The young bandit was losing a lot of blood, and soon after, he died. The stolen gold was never recovered and is still believed to be hidden near Staplehurst to this day. By the way, 3,000 oz of gold today is worth nearly 4 million dollars!

Around the same time as the train robbery happened, my great grandfather Frank who was 12 years old and living in Kladno, Bohemia made a trip to Germany and secretly boarded a ship to America. When it made it to New York City, he took a train to Omaha alone and settled 90 miles away in Brainard, NE. Frank later had 9 children. His son Joseph was my grandfather, who raised my father in Brainard. My family had relocated some 23 miles from his hometown in Staplehurst by the time I was born in 1973. If you want to learn more about Frank and his amazing story, read the book *Undocumented – A Young Man's Quest for the American Dream* that tells his story. It was written by my cousin Adella Schulz, his granddaughter.

Many years, ago I came across this story online about my hometown of Staplehurst which I had never heard before. As I dug deeper to learn more, reading many history books and articles, I discovered that the author W.C Jameson was the only source on this tale. I reached out to him about the authenticity and he assured me it was all true, that he had sources in notebooks buried in one of his sheds somewhere. It seems as though the documentation is also a missing treasure.

Jameson, W.C. Buried Treasures of the Great Plains. Little Rock, August House, Inc., 1998.

100 YEARS LATER

Although I don't believe in ghosts, I am certain my childhood home was haunted. I stayed away from that house as much as possible growing up. We moved in when I was 10-years-old. It sat on a corner lot, right across the street from the city park and village bar. The gas stove in the living room kept us warm and it had a window air conditioner for the summer months. There were 14 steep and creaky steps that took you upstairs where you would find two bedrooms separated by a hallway. One of the previous owners expended the house by adding an indoor bathroom and laundry room. The house had been re-located from just outside town in the country.

There were two doors that led to the upstairs. At night, these doors would slam open or shut on their own mysteriously. Growing up, I never told anyone about my fear, or the noises I heard while I was living in that house. I was afraid that if I let anyone know, they would make fun of me. Even worse, I didn't want to let whatever was there to know that I was afraid of them.

My bedroom was upstairs, but I often slept in the spare bedroom on the main floor. Going upstairs alone after dark was something I avoided. I believed that they came out after midnight, so I tried my best to fall asleep before the clock hit 12. If I was home alone after dark, I would leave the T.V. on and curl up in the middle of the bed completely covered up.

Looking back, I have conflicting memories and beliefs on what I experienced there. The mind can play tricks on you and make you believe things that are not real. This doesn't change the feelings I had at the time. I often went out with my parents or stayed over at a friend's house just to avoid being home alone.

My father would keep his hard liquor on the floor of our walk-in pantry. Sometimes when my parents were out of town, my friends and I would take shots of his Root Beer Schnapps or Vodka. We'd add water to the vodka to cover up what was missing or actual root beer to the schnapps. Mom also kept her retired purses in there. It was a great place to look for loose change when I wanted to play arcade games at the bar next door. One afternoon, my friend Bobby stopped by on his way to the Big Blue River to do some fishing. As I was scavenging through one of mom's old hand bags, he asked me to hand it over to him. He took some fishing pole string out of his tackle box and tied it to the handle of the bag. We both changed our plans for the afternoon and headed down past the railroad tracks just outside of town.

"Why are we sitting in the ditch?" I asked.

"Throw the purse over there right on the curb of the road," Bobby said.

I did as he asked; we then waited for someone to come into town. The first car came by and drove right past us.

"I could be playing Dig Dug right now," I said.

"Shhh! Here comes another car," he whispered.

The car started to slow down and came to a complete stop right behind my mom's purse. The driver got out, walked up to it, bent down and reached for it. That's when Bobby yanked the string, catapulting it back to us. The woman who thought she had scored a new purse was now embarrassed and ran back to her car and drove into town.

"That was AWESOME!" I yelled.

"HAHAHA," Bobby cried out.

We did this until the sun went down. Most victims took it well. Well, until old man Grigsby drove up.

Grigsby had farmed some land about a mile out of town. He had a reputation for not saying much. He pretty much kept to himself. I tried to get Bobby to reel in the purse when we realized who was coming, but it was too late. Grigsby stopped and ran up to the purse rapidly, grasping the purse before we could. Bobby and I both jeered the string at the same time. It flew out of his hands towards us. Soon after we heard a gun fire as he yelled in our direction.

"My grandfather knew how to take care of kids like you," He yelled holding on tight to his trusty shotgun.

My heart was racing, and we raced back into town down the side streets.

"What is he talking about?" Bobby questioned.

"I have no idea," I answered.

We cut the string and put mom's purse back where we found it and headed to the bar.

I always ordered a fountain "Spoke" a drink we had invented. Equal amounts of Coke and Sprite. They only charged us 25 cents a glass. I often called 1-800-GET-COKE and talked to the operators about our creation. They would humor me and send me Coke stickers in the mail. Am I really including a childhood recipe of mixing two soda's together? You bet, and I bet you'll try it next chance you have.

SPROKE

Equal parts of Sprite and Coke

SHALL WE PLAY A GAME?

In 1983, my sister Lori took me to see the Matthew Broderick movie *War Games*. This movie was what first got me interested in computers. Matthew's character was a high school kid that had a home computer. One of the interesting things he did was to hack into his school's network and change his grades. His computer also had a cool robot voice that talked to him. I was intrigued.

Whenever my mother made the trip to Lincoln, NE, I asked to go to one of the department stores because their electronics department had computers out and I was able to play with them. This was long before Windows, so everything was command line. You would have to type in a command and press enter to get the results similar to what became Microsoft DOS. I didn't know anything about how to operate them, so I mimicked what I saw in the movie. "Shall we play a game?" This always returned a syntax error. I didn't get it to play a game with me, but I had so much fun trying to figure out how they worked.

A few years later, my parents bought me a used computer (Commodore Vic 20) from a family friend who had upgraded to the now infamous Commodore 64. This computer was command line based. If I wanted to do anything with it, I would either type in hundreds of lines of code from a magazine or load saved software from tape. One of the tapes had a typing tutor and speed test on it. It would randomly generate a sentence from its database of names and actions, then, told you how fast you typed them.

Being curious, I edited the software and made it my own. I turned it into a drinking game I was going to play with my friends. The idea was to type at a certain speed with no errors or you would have to take a drink of beer. I figured out where the program stored the names and actions it used to build the sentences and I changed them to my friends' names and made the content more teenager based. For example, one of the sentences could have been:

"Stacy took a drive with Dan to the supermarket. "

Keep it in mind that these sentences were not put in as a complete thought. It was a database of names and actions. So, I first changed all the names to my friends'. Stacy turned into Sara and Dan became Eddie and so forth. I changed all of the actions. "took a drive" and others became "kissed" or "slept with" etc. Now the last part of the sentence "to the supermarket" became things like "at the park" or "in the back of a car". You get the point. After changing hundreds of phrases, the system was now creating random sentences that could be relatable to my friends.

"Kari kissed Brian at the park." It's too bad nobody ever saw my game. This was the first coding I ever did, even if it was just changing variable names. I figured out how to read code like a book and modify it to my liking. Fast forward to today. I've written complete payroll systems from scratch with timecards, PTO modules, overtime calculation, etc.

WASTED ROCK RANGER

During Christmas in 1989, my brother Les gave me his 1977 Plymouth Grand Fury. I was turning 16 a couple months later, and could not have been happier about the gift. I changed out the factory radio to a Kraco AM/FM cassette stereo system. This car was big, nearly 19 foot to be exact. One day in July, my cousin Jason and I decided to drive into town to get a burger at McDonalds. We had to drive over an overpass and just out of town to get there. When we got back in the car to head back home, I put in a tape of Great White playing one of our favorite songs at the time "Wasted Rock Ranger". Little did I know that years later I would be running Great White's website. I wasn't too impressed with the band themselves. Not that polite in my opinion. At any rate, I guess I didn't realize that on the way there, there was road construction. As I headed up the hill of the overpass, I had to act fast because of stopped traffic. I slammed on the breaks hoping to pull over to the side. I would look a bit silly but that was the only choice I had. Unfortunately, that plan backfired when the brakes locked up. I ended up hitting the car in front of us which in turn ran into the car in front of it. The car behind me also ran into me. All 4 cars were totaled. One of them, a cherry red mustang had just been driven off the dealer lot, about a half mile away. Nobody was seriously hurt but I got a letter in the mail the following week, stating I was being charged with careless driving. Our insurance company also cancelled our policy. When we went to court to enter a plea, my dad told me to plead not guilty. He said that the roads were not properly marked before the hill informing of the lane closed ahead. I automatically admit guilt in any situation till this day, so I didn't really agree with his instructions, but I did as he advised. The next court date came, and I went to the courthouse with Dad again. When we got there my attorney said that we could go home. The case had been dismissed because it had gotten mixed up with a distributing to the delinquency of a minor case. To this day, I don't understand what happened. I was out of a car and on high risk insurance until I was 25. I still like McDonalds hamburgers. I think it's because it's familiar. I did come up with my own seasoning that makes homemade burgers delicious. Try this next time you're grilling out or to use on hamburger pizza.

HAMBURGER SEASONING

INGREDIENTS

- 2 tablespoons of paprika
- 1 1/2 tablespoons ground black pepper (freshly ground preferred)
- 1 1/4 tablespoons of salt
- 1 1/2 tablespoons of dark brown sugar
- 1/4 tablespoon of garlic powder
- 1/4 tablespoon of onion powder
- 1/4 tablespoon cayenne pepper

DIRECTIONS

1. Mix ingredients in bowl
2. This recipe is an adaptation of one I found online. I primarily use it to season hamburger. I've also used it to season pizza and even French fries. It has a unique taste. Its spicy-sweet flavor is something very special.

NOTHING GOOD HAPPENS AFTER MIDNIGHT

"I have a bad feeling about this," my nephew, Wade, said to me.

Let me explain. I was an uncle four times before I was born. I guess I arrived a little late in my parents' life. Growing up, my siblings' kids would stay at their grandparents in the summers when school was out. Because of this, I was only close with a few of my nieces and nephews.

One night, in the late 80's after my parents went to bed, Wade and I quietly exited the house and went across the street to the park. That was our second stop. First, we met up with our friends, Donnie and Ginger who also snuck out of their houses and were waiting for us. We all walked a block up and started to throw little rocks at a window on the second level of my cousin Jason's house. There was no internet or cell phones back then. This was the only way to try to get his attention. Calling him would wake the entire house. This outing was not planned, so, to our surprise just a couple minutes later, he had gone downstairs and snuck out of the house to join us. We all headed together a couple blocks down to the park.

"What took you so long?" I asked.

"I was sleeping, and you almost broke my window!" Jason replied.

Staplehurst is only a town of 300 residents, but had three bars at the time. All of them on the main street and across from the park. The Sports Tavern was a great place to go and play Donkey Kong, Pool, and Pinball. At some point, we discovered that if you flatten a straw and slide it near the hinges of the coin slot, you could get free credits on Donkey Kong. You had to be smooth about it though and not draw attention to what you were doing. We didn't do it often because the game was placed in a high traffic area near the bathrooms.

It must have been a slow night because we noticed the Sports Tavern was closing early and the owners were going home. There was a little window above one of the side doors that they had left open. It was common knowledge to the kids in town that with a little boost, you could get into the building easier. It was still on the side of town facing the main street but in small towns there isn't much traffic late at night. Donnie and Jason had decided they were going to get into the bar and take some alcohol. This was when my nephew told me he didn't feel good about this. They had already started to walk across the street, so they were going to do it with or without a group vote.

The rest of us decided to head over to the swing set.

"Why can't we just play Pitfall! on your Atari?" Ginger asked.

"I don't think you are understanding what I did here," I replied.

"How is electronic typewriter a game?" Ginger continued.

Wade's swinging came to a quick halt.

"And how does your computer know all of our names, Ed?"

"I broke into the code and changed the names," I explained. I realized at this point that trying to explain further would not help anymore.

"You're in consumer math with me, I don't believe you." Ginger said.

"It doesn't really have anything to do with Math. I just figured it out."

As I was trying to explain my game, a pesky Monarch butterfly must have left its group just to come annoy me. I tried swatting it away, but it did not take the hint. It even hovered right in front of my eyes and I lost my train of thought. I was irritated and continued swatting at it until it flew away on its own. I felt relieved. Hopefully, it will tell its buddies I was busy.

At this point, Ginger had lost interest in our conversation. At the height of her swing, she had kicked her right shoe off to see how far it'd go. She wanted us to play along as we occasionally would, but Wade was too focused on interrogating me.

"So, we just type these magic sentences about us and if we make a mistake, we have to drink beer?"

I stopped swinging and took a minute to think about his question.

"Something like that. I haven't figured it all out yet."

"I don't like the taste of beer," Ginger said, getting up to retrieve her shoe, which had flown over towards the merry-go-round.

"Then, don't make any mistakes!"

Donnie was using Jason as a stepladder to crawl through a window located in front of the bar.

"It's so strange in here with the bar being empty," Donnie said as he was opening the main door to let Jason in. All of the chairs were turned upside down onto the tables, making it easier for the floors to be swept and mopped. The place was quiet, a huge change from the hustle and bustle of the bar during operating hours and it was lit up. All of the lights were now on.

"After you take a bottle of liquor, make sure to bring the bottle behind it up so that it doesn't look suspicious," Jason advised. This was the technique passed along by the first generation of the alcohol bandits.

You must give them credit, that was a smart technique. You would think that they would have wanted to get in and out, but they were taking their time.

"Does it void the warranty when you break into the code?" Wade questioned.

"No, it doesn't work like that."

After securing her shoe, Ginger sat on the Merry-Go-Round and jokingly said: "Do we have to wear computer gloves when typing on the machine?"

"Computer gloves? I don't think that's a thing, have you ever used a computer before?" I knew that Ginger was making fun of me at this point, but I didn't let it get to me.

Donnie had grabbed a to-go bag from behind the bar and began blindly filling it with bottles, when he heard something or someone towards the restrooms.

"What was that?" Donnie was worried that one of the owners had forgot something and came back. He quickly wondered how fast he could escape.

Donnie ran back towards the restrooms and back door when he noticed Jason had taken one of the quarters he found and decided to play a quick game of Pinball.

"We can come back tomorrow to play games; we need to get out of here."

"All right, this machine is out of balance anyways. Let me grab some beef jerky quick before we go, it's so good!"

Jason was right. It was stored in an open container right next to the jar of polish sausage that was soaking in vinegar water. He took the last piece and put it in his mouth, leaving it to dangle like a cigarette.

They locked the front door and decided to head out through the window. Donnie jumped out the window landing on his hands and feet like a dog. To his surprise, he was staring intofuz the eyes of the headlights of the county patrol. He got up and ran as fast as he could straight to my house which was a direct route about half the size of a football field. Jason was hanging half out the window and quickly jumped and ran behind the bar. They split up to cause confusion.

The rest of us hadn't even noticed the cop car, but we could see them darting in opposite directions out of the bar.

"I hope Jason remembers to grab some beef jerky," Ginger said.

"What is Donnie doing?" Wade said with excitement.

We all saw him dashing right to my garage which was on the same street of the bar. Since we didn't notice the cop, we walked casually back to my house and met him in the garage leaving the door open just a crack.

"Where's Jason?" I asked.

"There's a cop chasing him!" Donnie said.

Jason had hidden in a shed about twenty-five feet behind the bar. He soon noticed a flashlight moving around. The cop was so close that he could have touched the mustache and glasses on this face.

We all got really quiet quickly as we looked out the window towards the back of the bar. A couple minutes later, we noticed the cop car driving past my house and turning up the street. We didn't even notice Jason as he slid under the door into the garage like a baseball player sliding along the ground to reach home plate.

After some time, everyone left to go back to their own homes. So far, so good!

The next day after my nephew Wade had gone home, we all got together and had the nerve to go to that bar in question to play video games and pinball. We were using quarters they took that previous night to play Donkey Kong. There wasn't anything inside the bar that said anything about what had happened the previous night. One thing was sure though, I was not able to purchase any of their beef jerky because they were out of stock.

Sports Tavern sure did have good beef jerky. After I got my first smoker, I came up with this recipe so that I could have beef jerky whenever I wanted.

TAVERN JERKY

INGREDIENTS

- 4 tablespoons of ground black pepper
- 1 cup of soy sauce
- 1 tablespoon of cider vinegar
- 1 dash of hot pepper sauce
- 1 dash of Worcestershire sauce
- 2 lbs. sirloin cut into 1/2-inch-thick slices. (You can ask the butcher at your favorite supermarket to cut this for you).

DIRECTIONS

1. Marinate the meat overnight.
2. Remove meat from marinate, drain and pat dry all excess liquid.
3. Smoke meat for 2 hours. Keep the temperature under 200 degrees.
4. Transfer to a food dehydrator and turn on for 2-3 additional hours. It will be done when the jerky bends easily but does not break in half.

Note that: Beef top round steak, flank steak and rump roast are the best cuts for making jerky, the key is to use a meat with very little to no fat.

COMING-OF-AGE

I started dating when I was 16-years-old. I needed gas money to get around, so it was time to get a job. My friends and I all applied at the local pizza place, where everyone was offered a job except for me. Later that week, my study hall teacher advised me to apply at the Dandy Lion Inn outside of town. They hired me on the spot as a dishwasher. It paid $3.30 an hour, and I was happy to have work.

The bus boys would bring in tubs full of dirty dishes, plates, leftover food, and anything else on the tables. It was my job to rinse the plates off, soak the silverware, and throw away everything else. I also cleaned up all the cook's dirty dishes, pots, pans, and whatever else they used. I would slide the dishes into the dishwasher, and it would power wash everything. The dishes would come out hot. After they cooled off a bit, I would put everything away in its appropriate spot.

I had pride in my work, whether it was keeping my area clean, polishing the sinks, mopping the floor and anything else that was asked of me. Scott, the head cook at night, always had classic rock playing on the radio. This is where I developed an appreciation for Led Zeppelin and Eric Clapton. He pretty much kept it on that station, except when a certain Queen song came on. He'd sing, "We will, we will, change the channel."

I generally worked Wednesday, Friday and Saturday nights; while often picking up a day shift on Sundays. These were especially busy days because we had a buffet, and lots of folks would stop by after church. Sundays were so busy that we needed two dishwashers, which annoyed me because I preferred working alone.

About a year into my job, they were looking for a line cook. Scott asked me if I had ever cooked before. I said no. He responded with, "I'll teach you." and just like that I was done washing dishes. I felt important with this promotion and took it seriously. On the weekends, they staffed three of us on the line. Scott would cook all the steaks, prime rib, and everything else of importance. Dan was second in charge. I went to high school with him but didn't know him well. Working together changed that quickly and we became good friends. He took care of cooking hamburgers, chicken fried steaks, and making sandwiches. That left me. I quickly learned what parts of a chicken were dark or white. I made toast, fried the fries, and got all the plates ready for Scott to put his creations on.

This time in my life was really a coming-of-age story for me. The waitresses who wouldn't even notice me at school suddenly paid attention to me. I was also learning a skill that I would use for the rest of my life.

As the months went by, I earned the right to be the second line cook. I became good at making burgers and (sometimes), steaks plus I had more interaction with the wait staff. My confidence grew, and I felt like I was part of a new family.

Not long after, Scott decided to move on, and before I knew it, I was promoted to head night cook. All while I was still in high school. I felt good around there, and with my newfound confidence, I finally got up the courage to ask that waitress out. Her name was Robin, and we've been together ever since.

My favorite thing to make at the Dandy Lion Inn was Fried Iced Cream. I've modified it a little and it's become a family tradition to make on all major holidays in our home.

FRIED ICE CREAM

INGREDIENTS

- One container of Ben and Jerry's Cinnamon Buns Ice Cream
- (Regular Vanilla Ice Cream works fine too)
- 2 cups corn flake crumbs
- 1 cup graham cracker crumbs
- 1 tablespoon of sugar
- 1 pinch of cinnamon

DIRECTIONS

1. Combine corn flake and graham cracker crumbs into bowl.
2. Combine sugar and cinnamon into another bowl.
3. Make large size ice cream balls. Put on a flat tray and put back in freezer for at least 2 hours.
4. Pour two cups of corn syrup into a bowl.
5. Dip ice cream balls into the corn syrup covering them.
6. Coat the ice cream into the crumb mixture packing tightly and put back in freezer for at least an hour.
7. When ready to serve, put a small corn tortilla into a deep fat fryer or kettle heated to 350 degrees. Use a metal ladle to form a shell a few seconds after putting it into the fryer.
8. After cooking until crisp (About 1 ½ minutes), take out and dust with a cinnamon and sugar mixture. Drop an ice cream ball into the fryer for a short time. Typically, about 20 seconds until the coating starts getting crisp. The ice cream will not melt much at this point.

9. Place the Fried Iced Cream into the freshly made shell and add whipped topping and chocolate syrup if desired.

Note: You're putting ice cream in a fryer, so make sure your balls are completely frozen. You may start to see the ice cream melt a bit as you are frying. This is ok. You'll get the hang of it quick.

MY FIRST ORIGINAL SANDWICH CREATION

On one of my first nights cooking on the line, we had an order for a chicken salad sandwich. A simple order; two pieces of white bread with the chicken mixture spread on the sandwich cut in half and served on a small plate. I went into the fridge and got what I needed and filled the order.

One perk of working at the restaurant was free soda. You had to go out to the waitress station by the tables, where folks eat, to get it. After confidently filling the order, I went out to the floor. I did a quick scan of the customers to see how favorable their meals were that night. I noticed an elderly couple eating and I focused in on their conversation. The lady said, "I don't know why they call this a chicken salad sandwich."

Her words didn't really sink in until later that night when we were closing, and I was putting the perishables away in the fridge. The so-called chicken salad mixture I had used was labeled "Coleslaw." I have always kept that overheard conversation to myself, until now.

I was never a fan of traditional coleslaw, so a few years ago, I researched alternative ways of making it for a friend's baby shower I was catering. Below is my adaptation of Asian slaw. It's been a big hit at BBQ gatherings at my home.

ASIAN SLAW

MIX IN BOWL
- 1 tablespoon of minced ginger
- 3 tablespoons of olive oil
- 1/2 cup of rice vinegar (or rice wine vinegar)
- 1 Pinch of crushed red pepper flakes
- Salt and pepper to taste

TOSS TOGETHER
- 1/2 green cabbage thinly shredded
- 2 carrots, peeled and julienned
- 3 green onions, thinly sliced
- 1/2 Red Bell Pepper thinly sliced

DIRECTIONS
1. Mix in the sauce you made above.
2. Let it stand for 2 hours.

JUST BEFORE SERVING ADD IN:
1. 1/2 cup cilantro - chopped
2. Crispy Chinese Noodles for crunch (optional)
3. Black and White sesame seeds (optional)

SIGNS, SIGNS

After high school graduation, I enrolled in a community college studying Electronics. On the first day of class, they told us that statistically, only one third of the class would graduate. I didn't think that they had the best motivational speakers working there. We had assigned seating and were placed based on our high school grades. I was in the front row next to a couple other long-haired freaky people. They also called us by our last name. This wasn't a thriving place for me. There was a Van Halen concert on Easter Sunday 1992. I didn't make it to class the next day, or ever again at that school.

I quickly enrolled in the same College, my girlfriend Robin was going to and switched my degree to Computer Programming. I also cut my hair short for the first time since I could remember. It is quite sad but people had judged me without even knowing me. I wasn't allowed in Robin's house when we were first dating because her Dad (at the time) did not like me. I had never spoke to him so all he had to go off was my appearance. After my new haircut, I stopped to get gas at the place I had been going since I got my license.

When I went in to pay, the clerk asked me how I was doing.

This was the first time he had ever spoke to me. That's when I realized that perception is reality.

I did very well at the new college. After my first test in my first programming class, the department head pulled me into his office and asked me where I worked. I was still working at the restaurant. He said that I needed to quit and work there for him in the computer lab. I did as he suggested and worked there until I graduated and was even teaching classes at the college for a while after graduation.

I had just graduated from college and I could not find a job as a computer programmer. Robin and I were also expecting our first child. I had to find full time work fast, so I applied at a Mexican restaurant in Lincoln, NE as a food prep.

I got the job. Unlike the Dandy Lion Inn, I did not know anybody, and I wasn't thrilled to be there. To top it off, I worked the difficult shift of 6am-2pm. Most of the day, I made enchiladas. Trays and trays of them. In my high school days on the line, I would try to make each plate a piece of art and gave everything my all. This was different. More like a factory line. One day at lunch break, I used the pay phone in the lobby to call Robin. She informed me that my cooking mentor Scott had died. We decided at that time that Scott would be our sons middle name.

I made salsa once at this job. They made them in what looked like large plastic garbage cans. Nothing about it was fresh and I did not feel the love at all. We used cans of diced tomatoes and mixed in some corporate provided bag of seasonings. Lots of people ate there but scratch-made and fresh was not their thing. I only worked there for a few weeks before the college I went to, called and offered me a teaching job.

I have won a couple of cook-offs with the following salsa recipe. After making it at the restaurant and having no clue what I was putting in it, I had to come up with something better.

SALSA

MIX IN BOWL
- 2 cups diced tomatoes
- 4 tablespoons of diced jalapeno
- 3 diced garlic cloves
- 2 tablespoons of diced red onion
- 2 tablespoons of green onion
- 1 handful of cilantro chopped
- Juice of one small lime

At this point, you have the delicious Pico De Gallo. To turn in into salsa, add in 29 ounces of canned tomato sauce.

STILL ON SALSA

After I high school and just before college in 1991, I had an idea to make a fortune selling my mother's salsa recipe. I went to the local newspaper and paid to put an ad in the Thrifty Nickel in Nebraska and Iowa. The ad read:

Millie's Mexican Salsa. Send $1 and a self-addressed stamped envelope to Eddie Lance P.O. Box 61 Staplehurst, NE 68439.

Sadly, I did not get any inquires but it was one of my first business ventures ever. Recently, I found the original recipe while cleaning out my parents' estate.

MILLIE'S MEXICAN SALSA

INGREDIENTS
- 1 tablespoon of salad oil
- 2 large celery stalks, diced
- 1 large onion, diced
- 3 16 oz can tomato (or 12-15 fresh tomatoes peeled)
- 14 oz can chop green chilies
- 1/3 cup of corn syrup
- 1 tablespoon of Salt

In 3-quart saucepan, cook celery and onion in hot oil till tender. Add tomatoes, chilies, corn syrup, salt, and chilies. Break up tomatoes. Reduce heat and cook uncovered for about 45 minutes until mixture thickens slightly.

REUNION

The internet was just starting to become popular soon after I graduated college and I spent many years after creating web sites. I have made hundreds of web sites since the late 90s', but the very first one I ever made was the most successful. It was based around trying to raise awareness and to get my favorite band (Tesla of course) back together after they had broken up in the mid 90's. My web site, Teslaweb.com was getting over 1000 unique hits a day during its peak. This was before social media and Facebook and Myspace. I had a message board and chat room where fans would interact. The chat room was most active late at nights. I wrote the code so that all the conversations would archive so people could come catch up on the chats whenever they wanted to. I would also get emails from fans every day. It was mostly people asking me if I think Tesla would ever get back together. I always replied that anything was possible and suggest they check out the new bands they had formed. Then, one day out of the blue Brian Wheat (Tesla bass player) called me and said that everything I had been hoping for was coming true. Tesla was having a one-time reunion show in Sacramento, CA. He invited myself and my wife to come to the show as his guests and to stay at his place for the weekend. He advised that this may only happen once, so I should seriously consider flying out there.

We had just had our second child (Jenna) and did not have a lot of extra money laying around for airplane tickets. So, the next day, I put my prized pinball machine for sale on eBay to raise funds. It sold immediately, and we bought airfare to sunny California.

I had never flown before, so this was an interesting experience for me. We had to switch planes in Chicago. I remember us running frantically to find our terminal. When we landed at the Sacramento airport, I got on a pay phone and called Brian. He sent someone to pick us up and bring us to his house.

When we arrived at his historic Victorian house, the place was a bit chaotic. There were a lot of people wandering around. Tommy Skeoch (ex-Tesla) was in the backyard smoking pot with some girl that looked like a model. There was a makeshift control room where Brian's assistant was getting the guest list figured out. Tesla playing in their hometown for the first time in many years was a big deal and lots of friends and family wanted to be sure to get into the show. Brian showed us our room and we unpacked. Later that night, he took us out along with his manager and the rest of his posse to a nice restaurant. We went to bed that night in anticipation of the show the next day.

After getting up and ready for the day, Robin and I decided to go outside and walk around the neighborhood. Little did we know we'd lock ourselves out of the house. Rather than waking up Brian too early on the morning of his big reunion show, we had an early lunch at a Mexican restaurant right up the street from his house. They were making quesadillas on the flat grill in sight of where were sitting. They looked amazing so that's what we ordered. I hadn't ordered them much in the past because they didn't really do anything for me, but this changed my opinion on them. So much that after we got back to Omaha, I worked up my own recipe.

QUESADILLA

INGREDIENTS
- 1 can refried black beans
- Handful of fresh cilantro
- 1 red bell pepper, diced
- 2 bunches of green onion, diced
- 3 jalapenos, diced
- 10 tablespoon corn (fresh, frozen, or in a can)
- 1 package of flour tortilla's

DIRECTIONS
1. Mix all together and simmer for 5 minutes in stove with olive oil.
2. Spread black beans on one side of two flour tortillas.
3. Sprinkle Monterey jack cheese on top of one of the tortillas.
4. Using a spoon, spread vegetable mixture on top. 2-3 spoonful should be plenty.
5. Put second tortilla bean side down on top of the first.
6. Grill for a few minutes on each side or back in oven until crisp.

DIPPING SAUCE

INGREDIENTS
- 16 ounces of plain Greek yogurt. (You can also use sour cream.)
- 1 ripe avocado, diced.
- 1 packet of ranch dressing seasoning.
- 1 handful of chopped cilantro.

DIRECTIONS
1. Using a blender mix all together until smooth.
2. Refrigerate for at least 2 hours.

HELP DESK

I ended up working in an office doing computer tech support. The following was a typical day in my life at a job I did not enjoy.

"Have you tried rebooting?" I asked, trying my best to hang onto my rapidly fading patience.

I half-listened to her reply as I was going over the menu at tonight's choice of restaurant in my head. She was a sweet girl, but tech savvy wasn't on her resume.

"Let's start with that," I said. "Call me back with the results."

It was a canned response, but often, simply rebooting a computer fixes most problems. However, sometimes I gave people busywork just to stall them so that they left me in peace if only for a few moments. I reached for my coffee and took a moment to zone out from the white noise of voices, footsteps, ringing phones, and noisy printers.

"Eddie, line one," someone yelled.

I glanced at the light flashing on my extension and answered. Sure enough, it was a happier sounding co-worker.

"So, the reboot fixed it?" I asked.

I listened to a moment of happy gushing. The next morning, I was sure to find a Latte from the Coffeehouse down the street sitting on my desk.

"That's great," I said. "Glad I could help. Call me anytime you need me."

I sat back in my chair. While the design was kind to my lower back, there was nothing to be done about my environment. It was attractive enough. Our glass cubicles were state of the art. Sleek and contemporary, they formed an island in the center of room. We were surrounded by suits with appropriately impressive titles. I felt like a fish in an aquarium strategically placed for their entertainment. The suits often tapped on our glass from time to time to make sure we were still swimming around.

The printer was located a few feet away from my cubicle. The sound of the machine printing endless pages was like fingernails scraping across a chalkboard. I couldn't escape from that irritating sound any more than I could escape from my cubicle existence, and I was pretty sure some of my cube-mates felt the same.

I glanced toward the only window in my direct view. At least, it provided me with a glimpse of the world beyond, if you could consider staring at a tree much of a view. It blocked a good deal of light and seemed to be symbolic of the narrow scope of my world.

You know how when you used to play Pac-man and you finally devoured that last dot? You cleared the level and you got a second to relax? Then, a new round started. It was exactly the same, but a little harder. That was how I felt walking into that office every morning. The same but a little harder to get through. There had to more to life than this.

One of the suits left a pink post-it note on my desk to call somebody at another location. I stared at the writing, not quite able to decipher the name. After a few more moments struggling to read it, I called.

"What's wrong?" I asked.

"Is the internet down?" a feminine voice asked.

Though the voice was familiar, I still couldn't recall who it was.

"THE internet? I asked.

"I can't get into my webmail."

"You try resetting the router? Unplug it and give a moment, then plug it back in. Should work."

I stayed on the line until I heard the scuffling of the phone.

"I'm back up. Thanks."

Now that I had fixed THE internet, I was finally able to get back to business and call my wife to finalize our dinner plans for tonight. We were going out with our best friends to our favorite restaurant in Omaha. We always ordered the Spinach and Artichoke dip as an appetizer to share. After having it a couple times, I had decided (well, my wife had decided for me) that I was to re-create the recipe. We all agree that maybe we improved on it a bit.

SPINACH AND ARTICHOKE DIP

MIX IN BOWL
- 8 ounces of Cream Cheese
- One small container of Heavy Cream
- One small container of Sour Cream
- 1 tablespoon of Garlic Powder
- ½ cup of Parmesan Cheese
- ½ stick of melted unsalted butter
- 1 tablespoon of salt
- 1 tablespoon of pepper (freshly ground is preferred)
- 1 tablespoon of Red Pepper Flakes

Boil in water 5 ounces of frozen spinach with 14 ounces of canned artichokes for 10 minutes. Drain and pulse in food processor for a few seconds. Add mixture in bowl and mix.

Put in oven in an oven safe container on 350 degrees until crust forms. This will take about 20-25 minutes. You can put the boiler on for the last few minutes to get it to crust up more. Serve with Tortilla chips or sliced Italian Bread.

BETTY PANTS

"I'm sorry, Mr. Lance, but you are not on the list." A large bald man wearing a sleeveless black t-shirt that read "Security" in bold white letters said without looking up.

"Hey, maybe next time, kid." He continued with a smirk.

"Do you know who I am?" I thought to myself.

Maybe next time? I was getting mad. Great, this drunk with power idiot thinks that I'm trying to scam my way backstage. For the past few years, I was the driving force online talking about how Tesla should reunite and tour. Now, we're standing at will call in Kansas City on the hottest day of summer at the beginning of their Reunion Tour. It was almost like I got him that job on that day and he had the nerve to treat me rude.

I was trying to call Frank and Brian to let them know I was having issues with the passes, but my cell phone did not have service out in the middle of nowhere. Finally, after what felt like an eternity, Frank's guitar tech walked by and noticed me. He checked the list that the security dude was holding and noticed a "Betty Pants" on the list. Someone had written my name wrong. Everyone had a big belly laugh as me and my posse were finally walking to the back of the Amphitheater to meet up with the band.

We entered through the catering door where we immediately heard Frank talking sternly to a worker.

"This is embarrassing, man. Take care of them."

"Hey guys! Please help yourself to anything here. I have to get to sound check." Frank said to us with a smile.

The amount of food in the room was overwhelming. The show included Jackyl, Skid Row, Vince Neil of Motley Crew, and of course the headliners Tesla. We did not notice any celebrities at this point. The girls helped themselves to a couple chocolate covered strawberries as Frank had given us the go ahead. I didn't feel comfortable taking any of the food even though it seemed we were welcome to it.

Before too long, one of the road crew from Tesla walked in.

"What are you doing? Don't eat anything back here!" He said to us with anger.

"Come with me, stay in this room until it's time for the show." He shut the door behind us.

It was a small room right next to the back door that lead to the stage. It was noticeably cooler in this room. After a few minutes, it was downright cold.

There was a refrigerator stocked with water and beer and a cheese tray on a table.

We opened the door so that we could keep an eye on what was going on in the hallway.

We were all shivering after 20 minutes and wondering when someone was going to let us out of our ice-jail. The sounds of a chainsaw in the distance told us that the show had already started and Jackyl was playing their signature Lumberjack song.

We all agreed that since we had VIP passes, we might as well go out to the stage and watch from the side. The credentials could not score us chocolate covered strawberries, but it should get us a nice spot to watch the rest of the show.

As we stepped out to the hallway, it seemed to step right into the Motley Crew video "Home Sweet Home" where the band is walking from their dressing rooms to the stage. Except that it was just Vince. He was still in his prime and looked just like you would see him on TV with his hair blowing as if a fan was behind him. Robin almost ran into him as she stepped outside our jailcell. Vince stopped momentarily and gave her the Joey Tribbiani "How YOU doing'?" We waited for him to get a few yards ahead of us before exiting and finding our spot next to a couple of sound guys to watch the show.

It's always surreal watching Tesla play shows for me. They have been my favorite band since high school. I had seen them 4 times before they broke up in the 90's. Since then, I've been to over 60 Tesla concerts. Everyone one of the shows have been special in some way. This night was the 6th time. A few months prior, we flew down to Sacramento for the reunion show. This is the only time I watched the show from this side of the stage. It's an interesting view. You see a lot more of what's going on in the background with guitar techs and stagehands.

In between songs, Brian walked over and talked to us.

"Why do you want to watch from here?" he asked.

"The sound is so much better out there."

I understood what he was saying but couldn't get past the fact that he was hanging out with us during the show. The other benefit was if we had to use the rest room, we just walked backstage. No lines, air conditioning and free water were major perks of the position we were in.

After the show, we were invited to visit with the band backstage. I needed to talk to one of the band member's Tommy about a web site I was creating for him. He had some crazy ideas. Not a fan of interaction. This was before Facebook and Myspace and before message boards and chat rooms were popular for web sites. He wanted a page for a chat room on his web site, but it was just going to be a static page telling his fans to get a life. I made it up to look like it was a functioning chat room, but it really was nothing.

I didn't get the chance to talk business with Tommy that night. As we entered the room, we noticed a familiar face from MTV. It was Jesse Camp a rather popular VJ in the late 90's. He looked exactly as he did on TV. He had driven to Kansas City from New York City to see the Tesla reunion show. He was chatting with Tommy about acting when we arrived. It was a star-speckled night. We got photos with Jesse and talked to him for a bit. I noticed that Tommy was standing in the corner talking to Tesla's lead singer Jeff. I overheard Tommy saying something about his new web site, so I decided to join the conversation.

"Yeah, Eddie put it together for me. It's really cool!" Tommy said.

"Right on." Jeff replied.

"You got to check out the chat room. It's super interactive. You'll love it!" Tommy suggested.

"Oh, I will!" Jeff said enthusiastically.

After about an hour, we decided it was time to make the 2 and half hour drive back to Omaha. We walked out with Jesse Camp and his travel buddy. To this day, people still call me Betty Pants. I don't mind. It's a pretty good story.

After seeing backstage catering for a number of years, I had concluded that my mother's Mexican dip would be a home run at these shows for the stars.

MILLIE'S MEXICAN DIP

INGREDIENTS

- 16 oz. softened cream cheese
- 12 oz. Ortega Original Medium Taco Sauce
- ½ cup of diced tomatoes
- ½ cup of diced red bell peppers
- ½ cup of chopped green onion
- 1 cup of finely shredded cheddar cheese
- 1 handful of chopped cilantro

DIRECTIONS

1. Mix cream cheese with taco sauce until smooth
2. Spread mixture on a serving dish approx. ½ inch thick.
3. Top with all vegetables.
4. Serve with chips.

BORN AGAIN

One day at work, a couple of my friends invited me to go to lunch with them at this new place they had been frequenting and talked about with great excitement. I didn't realize until we got there that it was a BBQ place. I wasn't really a fan. All the BBQ I had previously in life were not that great and I didn't understand why people liked it. As we were parking, I was at the point of no return and just went with it.

To order, you took a piece of paper from the counter and checked what you wanted with a pencil. It reminded me a lot like Keno. Pick the numbers and hope they come in. I had no clue what to get so I just ordered the special "Burnt Ends" whatever that was and felt safe choosing a side of French fries.

A friendly face brought out our lunch a few minutes later. The fries looked good, but I kept looking around for ketchup. None to be found. I decided to use the BBQ sauce they had on the table. I don't care for BBQ sauce. All the store bought and even what you get at fast food chains didn't do anything for me. Same generic flavor everywhere. With an internal sigh, I dipped and put a fake smile on my face to my buddies on the table watching my every move. To my surprise, it was amazing. I almost regret using the word amazing because I'm not sure what descriptive words to use next as the story continues. That forced grin just turned genuine. I was starting to feel good about this experience. At the very worst, I will have had some top-notch fries. Then, there they were. The burnt ends. Little chunks of meat that had a nice deep color. It looked like they must have smoked these pieces for a long time. The smell was intoxicating. I hadn't experienced this before. It reminded me of a camp fire. I finally had to take a bite and get it over with.

This is going to sound weird but that moment in time was life changing. This was the tastiest thing I had even eaten. It was beyond amazing. It was like a reborn coming of age moment. I had a feeling of pure happiness and was instantly addicted.

For the next year, I would go there and eat at least 3 times a week. There were always big lines, so I tried to get there early. The Burnt Ends would run out quickly. This wasn't a huge deal because the brisket sandwich was almost as wonderful. Driving back to work after lunch was the best part, I was very happy and content. I would often call Robin and tell her how good I felt on the way back to the office. I'm sure she thought I was insane.

One day, it occurred to me that I needed to learn how to reproduce this. I started researching smokers and learned there are a lot of options. Propane grills using indirect heat, bullet smokers that seems to do a nice job using charcoal, and there are electric smokers where you set it and forget it.

NO MACHINES!

When Tesla started out in the mid-80's, a lot of other bands were using samples, sequencers, and drum machines. It was new technology and the flavor of the month. Tesla started using the term "No Machines!" in their marketing meaning they didn't use any "tricks" when performing keeping it all real. I felt the same about smoking meat. I wanted to be true and authentic to the art.

I decided to build a smoker made of bricks just like the 3rd little pig did with his house. He had wonderful results and I wanted the same. I found some plans on the internet and hired my childhood friend Alan to build it for me. On the first day of construction, I came up with the crazy idea to add a wood fired pizza oven into the design of the smoker. At this point I had no clue how they worked but I had recently read that wood fired pizza was something special. He approved the modified design and starting building.

The entire process took 3 months and over 1000 bricks. It turned out much larger than I had imagined and it was really a piece of art.

I wanted to make my first smoked creation simple, so we made smoked wings. I have not changed the process at all since the first time.

SMOKED WINGS

MARINATE IN BOWL
- Chicken wings
- Italian salad dressing

Cover and let marinate in the fridge for at least 12 hours. Drain the liquid and coat generously with rub. Put in the smoker for around 2.5 hours.

The CURTIS FARMS Collective

Got wood?
It comes seasoned, hard,
and ready for use.
We'll deliver it by the load.

QUALITY FIREWOOD PRODUCTS

SECONDHAND SMOKE

The whole idea behind smoked food is the smoke itself. No matter if you are using electric, gas, or charcoal you'll need at the very least wood chips to create the smoke. You can buy these at any general store or online. I personally like truly authentic things in general. I like old tube style musical instruments, the ones before circuit boards came about. I prefer to get the heat for my smoker with 100% wood. In fact, I prefer to start the fire with newspaper and smaller sticks rather than lighter fluid.

If you don't have the room in your smoker for a wood fire, you can use charcoal and sprinkle on wood chips. What kind of wood are we looking for? For smoking, you want a fruit wood. Apple, Cherry, or any other fruit works great. I get all my wood from one of my best friends Jesse from Curtis Farms located in rural Nebraska. They hook me up with mulberry wood. I was not familiar with this type of wood before getting a sample. It is very much like Apple wood. It smells wonderful while burning and I've used it exclusively for all my cooking for the past 10 years. It is basically part of my brand at this point.

I try to keep the fire at 225 degrees. If it goes down to 200 or up to 250 for a short amount of time that's fine. You'll want to babysit the heat checking it every 30 minutes or so. This is part of the fun though. Being outside with the fire and smoke. It's very calming and reduces stress. The smell is amazing. If I could bottle it up, I would sell it as cologne.

(8+3+1+1) = Rub

I really discourage any pre-packaged seasoning mix. It's just a combination of spices everyone already has at home. If you read the ingredients in your favorite taco seasoning, you'll notice that nearly half of the list is additives that you would never add on your own. Creating your own gives you the advantage of making your food original and unique. Something to take pride in.

Don't buy pre-mixed rub for your meats! Not only is it not yours, but it's expensive. You have everything you need in your kitchen now. My recipe is based off the 8+3+1+1 technique.
- 8 parts brown sugar
- 3 parts salt
- 1-part chili powder
- 1-part mixture of various spices

The last part is a combination of any spices, it's up to you. You'll see in the next page how I do it, but you can experiment and make it your own if you want.

I've made thousands of pounds of this over the years. The actual recipe calls for cups instead of parts, but I think of it as parts because this allows you to make as little or much as you need.

ED RUB BBQ SEASONING

MIX IN BOWL
- 8 parts light brown sugar
- 3 parts salt
- 1 parts chili powder
- 1 part consisting of equal amounts of
- black pepper (fresh ground preferred)
- garlic powder
- onion powder

This recipe works great with Brisket, Pork, Ribs, and Chicken, Seitan, and Tofu. Simply apply on the meat and rub it in. Now wrap it in plastic and let it chill in the refrigerator for 24-48 hours.

ONE MISTAKE CAN CHANGE EVERYTHING

Remember that incredible BBQ Sauce I talked about the day I became a born again BBQian? That was the most amazing sauce I've ever had. I often wondered how they made it. I was too shy to ask them though. Then, one day as I was enjoying a late lunch at the restaurant, I noticed someone walking around filling the containers up. It was a large one-gallon sized bottle and to my surprise it had a label on it. This must be a mistake; she should not have brought out the secret of their sauce just for anyone to see! But she did. The label read "Grandma Foster's" BBQ Sauce. I quickly wrote it on my hand with a pen. When I got back to the office, I did some googling and learned that it's made right here in Omaha, NE. I could even find it at the grocery store that we frequented. This was another life changing moment for me. It's truly the only sauce I buy. No need to make any from scratch. You're not going to get a recipe for BBQ sauce, this is perfection. By the way, you can also find it on Amazon. They only make two products. Mild and spicy. Get the spicy! You're welcome.

ERUPTION

"Open the fuckin' door! Open the fuckin' door! Open the fuckin' door!"

The chanting from thousands of fans crowding outside the auditorium resonated like a war cry before a battle. Immersed among the human crush, sniffing more than one whiff of weed, I felt the adrenaline pumping. It had been a stressful few months and my voice joined the others until the doors finally opened and the human stampede began.

I didn't really see much of the interior beyond a sea of bobbing heads. The main level was general admission, so those ticket holders had to beat the crowd to get seating as close to the stage as possible. The buzz of excitement and chatter was tangible as I made my way to the beer line. Because I had assigned seating on the first balcony, I didn't feel rushed and just enjoyed the hectic atmosphere. The line was short, but it still took a few minutes for me to reach the counter.

"That will be four tokens," said a blonde server.

"Tokens?" I asked.

"You have to get a wristband to verify your age," she said, indicating a line at another counter. "Then, you can get your tokens to exchange for beer."

While I felt flattered that she assumed I was underage, I wasn't thrilled at the prospect of standing in two more lines that reminded me of an airport check-in. Still, it was either that or nothing, so I waited to get my wristband and then got back in the endless token line.

"I'll take eight of your best tokens, please," I said to a stern-faced man.

"We sell them in groups of ten," he said without the slightest hint of a smile.

"I thought beers were four tokens each?" I asked in confusion.

"I have no clue what the beers go for," he said, showing me a wooden token. "I just know about these."

"Fine" I conceded.

I made a mental note to smuggle in some water bottles next time. By now, the beer line was practically to the door, but I had already invested too much time and I was determined to get my tokens' worth. When I finally reached the counter, I ordered a Miller Light from the blonde.

"We don't carry Miller Light," she said with a blink of her false eyelashes.

I couldn't help but glance at the prominent sign behind her proclaiming, 'Now Serving Miller Light!'

She didn't take the hint, but I did recall that the couple ahead of me had ordered a Bud Light, so I did the same.

The opening band was already on stage by the time I made it to my seat with one of the best tasting and most satisfying beers of my life. Threading my way past a forest of surging, swaying bodies, I opened my mind to the music and let it wash away the stress of the day.

The buzz for the headliners felt like electricity jumping through the rows. I was practically bouncing like a child waiting to open his Christmas presents when a red-haired, post-era hippie bumped against me.

"Sorry," she said.

"It's okay,"

The last time I turned away from the stage, I was standing beside an office jock wearing a well-worn and apparently original 1984 'Tour of the World' T-shirt.

"So how long have you been a fan?" she asked.

"Oh, uh, since high school."

"You from around here? What's your favorite song? I drove two hours to see this concert! Wouldn't have missed it for the world."

I felt a stirring of irritation. I didn't want to be rude, but I didn't particularly want to bond with Miss crazy woman at this time. With more than a little envy, I noticed a few people on the balcony jumping down to the main floor. In my younger years, I might have attempted it but now it seemed a little risky.

"Why are you here alone?" she asked.

Thank God the lights dimmed, and I could finally ignore her. The crowd erupted in an uproar as the lead singer appeared on stage.

"Good evening O…"

"Omaha," Miss crazy woman yelled at the same time.

I flinched. I could understand singing along with the lyrics, but this was plain annoying. By now the band appeared on stage. When the lead guitarist flashed his smile and began playing one of his infamous riffs, the only thing I focused on was the roar rising in unison from the audience. Everyone began moving and screaming along with the lyrics.

The lead singer spoke to the audience for a few moments before introducing the next song.

"This next song takes us back to 19…"

'"Eighty-six!" Miss crazy woman shouted.

This time she was about a second ahead of the singer, and her commenting continued into the song. I wondered bleakly if I was doomed to listen to her parroting during the entire show and feared that she would sing off-key lyrics out of time with the band. It was all I could do to keep from telling her something I might regret.

Then the lights dimmed, and the stage effects blazed to life. Miss crazy woman starting chanting, "Jump! Jump! Jump!" like a Marine drill sergeant. I couldn't take it any longer and jumped. Surprised by my own agility, I landed on the floor and got up. Nothing gets me down!

It was time for me to jump in and smoke my first brisket. This is how I've made brisket since day one. I read a lot of recipes and watched a lot of videos. I decided to keep it simple and the results have been outstanding. If you're going to go through the labor of love process of smoking brisket you may as well cook a large one. I've always bought one around 20lbs at Costco, Sam's Club, or my local market. You will get the same results with a small cut. Just adjust the smoking time down.

Try to pick a brisket that doesn't have a large amount of extra fat. But don't worry, most if it will render off during the smoke. Some people say to trim off some of the fat before cooking but I leave it. It keeps the meat moist and you can cut any excessive amounts off later.

Open the package and rinse off with cold water. Now apply a generous amount of rub. And yes, rub it in. Cover and refrigerate for 24-48 hours.

Place in smoker fat side up. This way the fat will render and marinate itself.

Smoke for 10-12 hours low and slow at 225 degrees. There are some common rules of cooking it until the internal temperature reaches 165 – 170 degrees but I've never monitored the temperature. It's more of a feel for me. You can certainly check it every few hours to see where it's at if you so choose. When you bring it in, let it sit for 30 minutes before cutting into it so that juices have time to redistribute. Now cut it into ½in slices as if you are making steaks. If you want to cut thinner and serve you can do that too. However, I then cut each steak into cubes and then pull each cube apart. It's so tender that this will be simple. Now you have it processed perfect for sandwiches. You may run into areas that are all fat or gristle. These can be discarded. If you are eating right away, enjoy! However, here is what I do. You can refrigerate the meat overnight or even a couple days. I then put a crockpot or roaster on low and add in a couple cups of beef broth. Add in the meat after it's warmed up. What I've found the secret to put it over the top is to add in more rub seasoning and mix. This will give each bite an extra kick of flavor. Let it all come together in there for at least an hour, stirring and taking sample bites occasionally.

There you have it, all the secrets to my brisket. I've never done it any different and it's turned out spectacular. Every single time.

SMOKED BRISKET

INGREDIENTS
- 20lbs of Brisket (or whatever size you like)
- ED Rub BBQ Seasoning

DIRECTIONS
1. Rinse brisket and season with rub. Cover and refrigerate for 24-48 hours.
2. Smoke for 10-12 hours at 225 degrees. You can buy smaller pieces of meat and decrease the amount of smoking time. I feel like if you're going to do it, do it and smoke a large piece.
3. To make burnt ends, simply cut the brisket into cubes after 8-10 hours (let brisket rest for 15-20 minutes before cutting). Place in disposable aluminum foil pan(s). Do not stack. Add beef broth covering them 3/4ths. Sprinkle a generous amount of ED Rub on top. Smoke for another 2 hours flipping them at halfway point. You can them toss them in BBQ sauce if you like.

FRIED INTERNET ON A STICK

I've created hundreds of web sites over the years. The first one was called "Operation Reunite Tesla". It was a campaign to try to let the band know that they still had fans and that they were wanted. Because of the success and recognition of that site, I started a web site company and ran it for 10 years. We did web sites for numerous businesses, national bands, and radio stations.

The Nebraska State Fair was not looking for a new web site. We thought that they needed one though, so we created a mockup landing page and drove down I-80 to Lincoln where their offices resided. Oh, we didn't have a meeting scheduled either. I had the idea of playing the part of a state fair enthusiast, so I was wearing blue jeans, a t-shirt, and a ballcap on backwards. When we walked in and asked to speak to the "one in charge of this place", I was snacking on cotton candy. The fair boss came out and didn't know what to think of us. We asked him if we could show them a demo of what their web site should look like, and I offered him some cotton candy. He passed on the candy but said if we were quick, we could show him right there in the hallway. I proceeded to hook up our overhead projector and beamed it on the wall. A small crowd gathered during this time. All we had was a flash animation of a tractor driving in a corn field. On the back of the tractor was a sign that read "State Fair or Bust". There was some banjo music playing in the background as well.

When it was over everyone started clapping and we left with a signed contract. Later that year, we went to a press conference that included media from around the state. Our web site had won an award for best fair web site in the country.

I ran their web site for a number of years. They would email me updates to post on the site. One day out of nowhere with no reasoning or explanation they sent a PDF attachment to post. It was a press release asking for web site designers to submit their resume for the open job of maintaining their web site. I found it funny, but I did not apply.

State Fairs are known for their unique foods. Funnel cake, Cotton Candy, Deep fried Oreo's, and so on. Here is my take on a stuffed baked potato. This one is a game changer.

STUFFED BAKED POTATOES

Start with 5 large potatoes. The big brown ones commonly used for baked potatoes work best. You can either microwave these until cooked fully (15 minutes) Or put them in the oven for about 45 minutes at 350 degrees.

Once you got them fully cooked, cut them all in half. At this point, you can hollow out all potato meat into a large mixing bowl. Take out just about all the potato, leaving only the skin and just a little bit of potato. Don't worry if they get flimsy on you. We'll re-build these later and they will take shape again.

Now you can start adding the amazing ingredients that make these so special. I like to start by adding a stick of REAL butter. Don't use any substitute. We are going for flavor here and there is nothing like real butter! You can melt it first if you like however the heat of the potato meat will generally melt the butter for you.

Now add:
- 8oz Cream Cheese
- One Small Tub of Sour Cream
- One medium bag of Shredded Cheddar Cheese

I don't measure the dry ingredients; you can't screw this recipe up if it's made with love.

Add approx..

- One tsp Salt
- 1 ½ tsp of **FRESH GROUND PEPPER**. Don't use anything but freshly ground pepper. This goes for anything that calls for pepper. There is a lot of great flavor in freshly ground pepper.
- One teaspoon Garlic powder (not garlic salt!)
- ½ teaspoon ground oregano
- ½ cup chopped chives
- ½ cup half and half. This is another secret that works with making mashed potatoes. Don't ever use milk, use half and half. Not only will it will make your potatoes whiter, it will add tons of flavors.

Now use a whip or your electric mixer to get all the ingredients combined. You're going for a nice thick substance. The half and half may make the mix a bit soupy. In this case just add some instant potato flakes. I like to use a flavored mix like 3 cheese or garlic. There is no shame in using instant along with real potatoes, nobody will ever know. When your mix is at the desired thickness, it's time to re-create the potatoes. You can either use a spoon or a fancy pastry bag if you want to make them look extra nice. Either way is fine. Make them as large or small as you like.

The next step is optional but it's what puts these over the top. Take 6-8 slices of raw bacon and cut them into small cubes. Add in 4 cloves of garlic chopped up along with ½ of a medium sized onion chopped up as well. Put this all into a pan and fry it up until the bacon is just short of being crispy. It's ok to sample these bacon bits at this point, they taste like nothing you've eaten before.

Sprinkle the bits on top of each potato and put these in the oven on 350 degrees for about 25 minutes. You will never buy store made twice baked potatoes again and your friends and family will love you forever.

CANCER SUCKS

"**I**'m not going to die."

My brother said this to me numerous times when he was going through chemo-therapy and radiation. I believed him at the time. This was the first time I had someone close to me get cancer. It was a real dark time for our family. Holidays were big gatherings for us. Christmas and Thanksgiving were times when everyone came together at my parent's house. Since I was a young boy, I've looked forward to these events. There was always lots of food and good conversation with my siblings. My brother Les would often try to get me to go hunting, fishing, or camping with him. He said he needed to teach me "something". I wasn't really into the outdoors though, so that never happened. I remember him coming to Christmas numerous times excited to try whatever food I had made that day.

On the elevator at Harrah's Casino about to meet my business partner. We had been planning to start a food truck for a couple months and decided to finalize the plans for Smoke-N-Pizza when my brother called to let us know that he was going to stop treating his cancer. He also mentioned his plans of having a big gathering for Christmas one last time and asked me to make his favorite food that I made: Southwest Egg Rolls. I agreed, but I knew what all of this meant. The business meeting that night was bittersweet as this was the beginning of something exciting, but it was also the beginning of the end for my brother.

Christmas came, and I prepared 100 egg rolls for what was to be the last family gathering with everyone. I sat next to him for part of the day, showing him photos of the food truck and the portable pizza oven. He was interested and proud of what we were doing.

Soon after the Christmas party, he decided he wanted to stay at the care center in his hometown. We would come and visit him as much as possible on the weekends. He'd often have *Diners Drive-ins, and Dives* on the TV. He had never tried my wood-fired pizza; we were waiting for a good-weather weekend for me to bring the portable oven to town and make him some. That day came but just a couple days too late, as he had stopped eating all together. We still made the pizza, and the rest of the family was able to enjoy it, but he couldn't.

During the last week, he was completely unresponsive. I took the week off from work and stayed with the family as we awaited the inevitable. The first day when Robin and I went to visit, his room was completely quiet and peaceful. There was pretty music playing. He was there but not there. As we left the room and closed the door, I hugged Robin and broke down crying. This was probably the only time Robin has seen that from me. I try to stay strong in these moments as to not make anyone around me sad from seeing me sad.

Later that week, after I got home for the day from visiting, I was catching up on my email. Suddenly, the song "Fishing in the Dark" (*You and me go fishin' in the dark...*) started playing very loudly on my computer. I thought it was strange, and I showed Robin that no other window or program was open—it was just playing this song. About an hour later, my brother's wife called us to let us know he had died about an hour earlier.

I haven't made southwest eggrolls since that last Christmas. Here is the recipe.

SOUTHWEST EGGROLLS

INGREDIENTS
- 2 tablespoons of extra virgin olive oil
- 1 skinless, boneless chicken breast
- 2 tablespoons of chopped green onion
- 2 tablespoons of diced red bell pepper
- 1/4 cup of black beans
- 2 tablespoons of frozen chopped spinach
- 2 tablespoons of fresh diced jalapeno peppers
- A dash of salt
- A pinch of ground cayenne pepper
- 3/4 dub shredded Monterey Jack cheese
- 2 tablespoons of chopped cilantro
- 1 tablespoon of ground cumin
- 1 tablespoon of chili powder
- 1 pkg. Egg roll wraps (12)

DIRECTIONS
1. Cut chicken breast into 1-inch cubes.
2. Sautee chicken in EVOO with green onion, chopped spinach, peppers, and all dry seasoning until chicken is fully cooked.
3. Add in black beans, cheese, and cilantro. Mix well until cheese is melted.
4. Add one large tablespoon of mixture to each wrap and roll.

Folding the egg rolls is tricky at first. I suggest watching a YouTube video of someone doing it as a reference. The visual is very helpful. You will catch on in no time.

I always have a bowl of water that I dip my finger in. Then, I run my finger along the corners of the eggrolls to seal them.

You can then deep fat fry, bake, or air fry the egg rolls until they turn golden brown.

My homemade avocado dip has always been a favorite for dipping.

AVOCADO DIP

INGREDIENTS
- 16 ounces of plain Greek yogurt. (You can also use sour cream.)
- 1 ripe avocado, diced.
- 1 packet of ranch dressing seasoning.
- 1 handful of chopped cilantro.

DIRECTIONS
1. Using a blender mix all together until smooth.
2. Refrigerate for at least 2 hours.

DIVINITY

For many years, my brother made and brought his divinity to our family get togethers. It was always well received. Here is his recipe:

INGREDIENTS

- 1 cup pecan
- 2/3 cup of light corn syrup
- ¼ cup of water
- 2 2/3 cups of sugar
- 2 egg whites
- 1 tsp. vanilla extract

DIRECTIONS

1. Using a blender, chop nuts. Put corn syrup, water, and sugar in medium saucepan over medium heat. Stir until sugar is dissolved. Bring to a boil and cook over moderate heat, without stirring, until mixture reaches 260 degrees on candy thermometer. In large mixer bowl, beat egg whites until stiff peaks form. Continue to beat while slowly pouring hot syrup in a thin stream into egg whites. Add vanilla and continue to beat until mixture forms very stiff peaks and loses its gloss. Quickly fold in chopped nuts. Drop mixture by rounded teaspoons on wax paper.

DON'T LEAVE THE RESORT

Interesting story concerning the first time I ever hailed a cab; long before the convenience of Uber, which would have saved us a lot of grief. My wife and I were in downtown Cancun, Mexico, just the two of us. I got the cabbie to stop and asked him to take us to our resort. He just looked at me with a blank stare and after what seemed like forever, he spoke.

"I am sorry, I do not speak English".

It sounded like perfect English to me, but it seemed those were the only words he knew. We were lost in Mexico without a cell phone, identification, a limited supply of cash, and not a word of Spanish language fluency. There was a ring of sweat halfway down my shirt and without a watch we had no idea of what time it was.

The conversion rate from pesos to dollars is a lot like time duration in Mexico. Ten minutes seem like an hour. When you have no phone, no watch, and no responsibility, time goes on forever.

Just two hours earlier, we were at the resort sipping on a Pina coladas on the beach. We thought we'd walk across the street to the flea market. It was off the resort yes, but only a few blocks.

After walking a good 5 minutes, I wondered why we hadn't found the market yet. We saw it on the way to the resort the previous day.

"Let's just keep walking, it has to be close now," I said.

We finally found it. In retrospect, I don't think this was the same one we remembered, but so excited to finally find something we went in.

It was like the circus in there. Mexican Carnies would ask you to come in just to, "take a look," and everything they had for sale was only a dollar. This had piqued our interest of course. We ended up buying a couple of t-shirts, a decent deal I suppose.

As we finished shopping, we turned around to return to the resort, so we could continue our drinking. However, nothing looked familiar on the walk back, but of course nothing in Mexico was familiar to newbie's like us. We both mentioned several times we should be back by now but kept walking. A little while later, we asked a man standing on the corner if we were close to our destination. He said that we were walking the wrong direction and should consider taking a bus or taxi. Somehow, we got turned around. Those carnies must have messed with our minds.

At this point, we were tired from walking but turned around and started doing it again discussing what the hell happened. After a while, we decided to jump on the city bus. When we entered, we asked the driver to take us to our resort and he said, "Sure, sure." The driver pointed to where we were supposed to put the money. We dropped in $2 and had a seat in the 2nd row.

The bus was going slow at first, but we were so relieved to finally be sitting that we didn't focus much on time. Five minutes later, when they picked up speed, we became concerned about where we were going. The couple behind us noticed and asked us where we were headed. We told them, and they said we were going in the right direction and that it was about 15 minutes away. That didn't seem to make sense to us, but since we didn't have any concept of what time it was or how much time had passed.

We continued. The longer we stayed on the bus the more we were getting concerned. I turned around to ask the young couple if they were sure. When I looked back, there were two older women sitting in their seats, with the couple nowhere to be found. This is when I started to become worried. At the next stop, I asked the bus driver where our hotel was, he put his left hand on his head slapping it, kind of like saying, "Oh no," and he pointed the opposite direction. We quickly got off realizing we were in the bad part of town, and quickly headed even further down the road.

As we crossed the street to head back the other direction, I realized that everyone so far had led us in the wrong direction. We were in the wrong part of town, no cell phone, no identification, and very little cash. We were literally lost in Mexico. This brings me to the nice man in the cab. At this point, I was sure nobody spoke English and that we were in a good amount of trouble. I pulled myself together as my wife started crying. I said to her this is not the place to cry, somebody is going to realize something is up and take even more advantage of us. She put on her sunglasses and we walked up another couple of blocks until another city bus stopped. We got on and asked for directions to our resort. He assured us to get in and give him the money. We did.

Twenty minutes later, I noticed a sign that said our resort was in the direction we were going. At the next stop, we got out and hailed a taxi driver. He spoke perfect English and told us he would take us there for $4. I knew we were close, and we were not trusting anyone at this point. We declined and looked around for landmarks. Soon, we saw familiar territory- the flea market. This time we noticed more details and were able to reverse our footsteps and get back to our room quickly. Soon after we ordered some room service including one of my favorite Mexican dinners, enchilada suizas. I have always had a hard time ordering this because of how it's pronounced. Because of this, my version is named it after one of my favorite Tesla songs.

ENCHILADA LIL' SUZI

INGREDIENTS
- 2 slow roasted chicken breasts, shredded
- 8 ounces cream cheese
- 8 ounces heavy cream
- 8 ounces sour cream
- 4 tomatillos
- 1 Jalapeno pepper
- 1 Anaheim pepper
- 1 Poblano pepper
- 1 garlic clove
- ½ Small Onion
- 1 package of flour or corn tortillas (I prefer flour)

DIRECTIONS
1. Mix chicken with softened cream cheese. Set aside.
2. This is the fun part. Place the tomatillos, peppers, onion, and garlic on a baking sheet. Drizzle oil over them, add salt and pepper. Now roast in oven on 350 degrees for 20-25 minutes. You can mix up the peppers using any of your liking just make sure they are green.
3. Let them cool for 5 minutes and put in an electric mixer or food processor until it has a nice salsa consistency. Add in heavy cream and sour cream. Mix well.
4. Warm tortillas in microwave to soften them up. Now fill each with chicken mixture and roll up. Place them all in a backing dish. Pour tomatillo sauce on top. Back for 20 minutes at 350 degrees.

RYAN SCOTT LANCE

It goes without saying that my father is constantly thinking of new recipe ideas, or ways he could add his own unique spin to classics. Growing up, it felt like every other week he'd have a new invention for us to try. Out of all the different things he made over the years, his Over-Baked Sandwiches were always a personal favorite of mine. Although he's made them countless times, and I could easily write about how this dish has impacted me, or how my admiration to my father's craft has taught me to appreciate the culinary arts. I'd much prefer to take this opportunity to share one particular story that showcases another facet of my father's personality.

I was born in the small town of Seward, Nebraska. Although my parents moved to the big city of Omaha when I was around 3-years-old, we often spent our summers and holidays visiting Seward, so we could spend time with my grandparents. Moving back-and forth between the two towns was bizarre. Where in one town you'd have massive IMAX cinemas, with multiple screenings, each able to fit nearly one hundred people, in the other you'd have a small one-screen cinema that shares a wall with the local post office.

Flashback to the year 2001, where my naive 6-year-old self was greatly anticipating the release of Spider-Man. Being a scrawny and pasty child (I wonder who I got those genes from), I always identified with the character of Peter Parker and loved reading his comics and watching Saturday-Morning cartoons based on his adventures. The idea that any person; regardless of their gender, age, or background, could be behind that iconic red and blue suit was genuinely inspiring to me. So, obviously, seeing a major motion picture adaptation based on him, filled my younger self with more enthusiasm than I knew what to do with; I needed to see it as soon as possible.

Unfortunately for me, during the week of its release, my family was planning to have their monthly trip to Seward and I was told we couldn't see the film until we returned home to the big city. However, one night as everyone was blowing up air mattresses at my grandparent's house, my father surprised me by taking me to a midnight screening of Spider-Man at Seward's tiny theater. I remember that evening clear as day, him purchasing our father-son tickets at the box office, getting us a big bucket of over-priced popcorn, and finding a pair of seats that weren't too worn or stained with soda. As the lights started to dim, the crowd became silent, my little heart was pounding with excitement. Then, my father leans over to whisper something to me before the film began.

"You know, I heard that half-way through the film they drop spiders down from the ceiling for a more authentic experience."

I was horrified. I quickly looked up to the ceiling, expecting to see a bucket of loose spiders hanging over my head, tied to a rope with an eager teenager ready to traumatize me. However, it was too dark to see anything, as the Marvel logo appeared on screen, I quickly accepted my fate.

Needless to say, that didn't happen, and my father is a liar in the weirdest way imaginable. He's lucky I found the movie to be amazing at the time or else I'd probably have cripplingly arachnophobia to this day. Moral of the story is, my dad has a weird sense of humor. But, hey, at least he can make a good sandwich, right?

OVEN-BAKED SANDWICHES

INGREDIENTS
- 1 lb. Ground Chuck
- 1 Small Onion (diced)
- ½ Cabbage (chopped)
- Salt and Pepper to taste
- Frozen Yeast Dinner Rolls (32)

DIRECTIONS
1. Cook ground chuck on medium high heat while adding in onion, salt, and pepper. You'll want to add a little more pepper than what you would normally think is needed. It won't taste over peppered after baking. After a few minutes, add in cabbage. It will look like a lot of cabbage compared to the meat, but it cooks down. Reduce heat and continue to cook for 20-25 minutes until cabbage is fulling cooked and highly reduced.
2. Drain liquid and put in a food processor. Pulsate several times until everything is one consistent size. Set aside.
3. This part can be done ahead of time. Arrange frozen balls on a baking sheet and let them rise about 50% in size. This time will vary but it's approximately 1.5 hours.
4. Flatten a ball and stretch out in your hand so that it's around the size of the palm of your hand. Now take a heaping teaspoon of your meat mixture and place it inside your dough. Make sure that the dough is stretched out

large enough to have extra width on all sides. This way you can now fold from side to side enclosing the meat completely. Form the dough into a circle and place back on backing sheet. Repeat this process for the rest of the balls.
5. Let the balls rise at least another 50%. Meanwhile, preheat oven at 350 degrees.
6. Bake for 15 minutes. Take out of oven and spread melted butter all over each roll. Put back in oven for 3-5 minutes until they turn golden brown. Take out of oven and let it rest for 5 minutes.
7. These can be frozen and rewarmed in the microwave with great success.

When I was growing up, once a year my mother, along with her sisters and other family members would make dozens of these all day and freeze them to eat throughout the year. I had not yet acquired the taste for them, so she would fill the dough with mozzarella cheese and 2-3 pepperoni's rather than the meat. I absolutely loved them, and I still do. Try making this adaptation yourself. You can also make homemade dough if you would like. I've done it this way many times too. Buying the frozen balls just saves time and doesn't take away from the results.

BACKSTAGE PASS

GUNTER GLIEBEN GLAUTEN GLOBEN

When I write a new screaming guitar riff-like recipe, I release it on social media to see what my fans think. It's a ritual for me. I give them backstage meet and greet access to interact with me so that I know if I created the next big thing or if I should just stick with the hits. Food is my music. The fans are those who eat it up.

One day while I was foodstagramming, I got a phone call from one of the guys from Tesla, Brian Wheat.

"We're coming to Omaha on the Def Leppard tour. Bring me some BBQ!" Brian demanded.

"What do you want? Brisket?" I asked.

"No, Phil Collen got me into eating Vegan. Make some Vegan Burnt Ends," he suggested.

Every time Tesla comes to Kansas City, Brian gets Gates BBQ. I often join him after their concerts. Gates does not offer vegan options.

I had been wanting Brian to try my smoked meats for quite some time. Now that the opportunity presented itself, I had to rethink everything. I never ever smoked anything that didn't come from a cow, pig, or chicken. This isn't what I do. It was like asking Tesla to play a Polka after 30 years of rock and roll.

"No problem, I got this," I lied.

Later that day, I started to google how I could pull this off. A few weeks later, after getting a game plan, I had some friends over to get some feedback. I ran into a lot of opposition. I had a hard time even getting them to try it. It looked like and had the scent of meat, but they could not wrap their heads around it. Fortunately, my daughter who is a vegetarian had no issues giving it a try and she fell in love. I still make these for her almost every time I smoke a real brisket.

My first arena concert was at the Civic Auditorium in Omaha. I saw all the legends there. AC/DC, Aerosmith, KISS, Motley Crue, Guns n Roses, and so on. The Civic was torn down some years ago but the iconic name will stand forever. These days, Auditoriums have sponsors. Since it opened in Omaha, ours has changed names 3 times. The night of the Def Leppard, REO Speedwagon, Tesla concert, it was called Centurylink Center (not as remarkable as the Civic Auditorium). General admission concerts are also a thing of the past. We used to camp outside the Civic, hours before the doors opened, so that we could get as close to the stage as possible. You pay premium prices for those seats these days.

Tesla hit the stage at 6:50pm. This was the first time in 10 years since they had played in Omaha. They did a great job as always. I had seen them play over 50 times now, so there were no surprises; just the top-notch quality that I was accustomed to. Some 20 minutes after their set, I got a text from Brian to meet him on the floor. Security is always tight, so I was a bit nervous about gaining access to the floor. I decided not to do a stop and chat with the woman guarding the door to the floor and just walk right past her pointing at my "Guest" pass that had no power to get me on the floor. She didn't stop me, so I guess acting like I was important did the trick.

Brian escorted us backstage and we went into the catering room. It's always a surreal experience backstage at shows like these. We passed by Joe Elliot (Def Leppard singer) talking to a group of folks and walked right past Rick Allen (Def Leppard drummer) as we entered the catering area.

We sat with a couple other members of Tesla and their road crew. Brian unpacked the food and laid it out on the table like a thanksgiving feast. I was surprised that everyone was digging the food. They didn't even ask what it was before taking a fake meat bite, dipping it in the sauce I had included. One of them even mentioned it was better than the spread the arena had set out for them that day. I thought everything on the buffet looked great, but I was happy to get the positive reviews.

Reo Speedwagon who was second on the bill that night had already started their set and we could hear them from where we were sitting. Frank Hannon (Tesla) knew I was a fan and asked me if I wanted to go watch them side stage. Of course, I agreed, and we went out there. Another surreal moment for me was when we were standing just a few feet from the stage on the side behind the barriers of the crowd. Frank was air guitaring and the band was looking over at us giving Frank the "what's up" head nods. I had nothing but smiles by the end of the song when Frank took a moment to take a selfie of us watching the band.

BURNT VEGAN ENDS

INGREDIENTS
- 1 ½ cup vital wheat gluten
- ¼ cup nutritional yeast flakes
- 1 cup ice water
- 1/3 cup low sodium soy sauce
- 1 tablespoon of ketchup
- 2 cloves of garlic, minced
- 1 teaspoon of finely grated lemon zest
- 2 teaspoons of paprika
- ¼ teaspoon of cumin
- 1 teaspoon of freshly ground black pepper
- ½ teaspoon of chili powder

DIRECTIONS
1. Mix all dry ingredients in a bowl
2. Mix all wet ingredients in a bowl
3. Mix the wet together with the dry and stir gently until you form a soft dough. With your hands, knead gently for 2-3 minutes.
4. Rip apart ½ inch section of dough and form it into cubes with your hands. Repeat with all dough.
5. Boil 6 cups of vegetable broth (my favorite is Seitenbacher Vegetarian Vegetable Broth and Seasoning) and then turn heat down to medium. One by one, drop each cube into the pot.

6. Simmer for 15 minutes. The cubes would have doubled in size and be fully cooked at this time. Drain and place aside.
7. Coat each cube lightly with BBQ Sauce (My favorite is Grandma Fosters but if you are going for 100% Vegan, see recipe below).
8. Dust a generous amount of rub all over each cube.
9. Smoke for 2-3 hours at 225 degrees.

My secret BBQ Sauce has always been Grandma Fosters however it's not Vegan, so I had to come up with something in these instances where it had to be. After experimenting a number of times, here is what I came up with.

BLUES VEGAN BBQ SAUCE

INGREDIENTS

- 2 cups of ketchup
- ¼ cup molasses
- 1/8 cup apple cider vinegar
- 2 tablespoons of olive oil
- ½ cup of blueberry jam
- ¼ cup of maple syrup
- 1 tablespoon of soy sauce
- 2 cloves of garlic (minced)
- 1 tablespoon of paprika (regular or smoked)
- 1 tablespoon of dried oregano
- 2-3 dashes of hot sauce
- Pepper to taste

DIRECTIONS

1. Mix in saucepan
2. All together and stir. Simmer for 15-20 minutes on low heat.

CZECH ONE TWO

In 1949, at the age of 15, my Dad and his best friend Lou had a job in Sioux City, Iowa. They were living near Seward, Nebraska and had no way to get there. A friend of theirs advised them to jump in a boxcar train and in the morning, they would be in Sioux City. They took his advice and got in. There was a bunch of hard paper in there, so they covered up with it to keep warm and probably not to be noticed. The next morning, they arrived in Sioux City and put in a full day's work.

In my early 20's, I once helped my dad with a cement job. My task was to shovel one ton of sand out of the back of his truck and hand him cement blocks as he needed. It was the hardest work I'd ever done. He did this type of thing every day for most of his life.

After Dad's funeral in 2014, some of the family came back to my parent's house and spent some time in his garage. A lifetime collection of tools was in there just as he left it. This was where he spent a lot of his free time working on bicycles and mopeds among other things. I found a box of old cassette tapes that were labeled with names of bars that were all familiar to my childhood.

After the service that day, friends and family were talking in the church hallway and I was told the story of how I came to be. Dad had assembled a couple of friends and put together a Polka band. As the story was told to me, he was so excited after the first practice that he came home that night and I was born 9 months later. Dad was a founding member of The Seward Polka Dotts. I went to his shows almost every weekend until I was old enough to stay home alone. Polka was all I knew until seeing a KISS movie on ABC when I was 5 years old. Most Polka bands had a Tuba player, but Dad played a double neck guitar. Six string on top and Bass which he played on Polka songs on bottom. They were the best Polka band I've seen still to this day. They also threw in some country where Dad got to sing lead. He did Johnny Cash very well. I took the tapes I found home for review.

The quality of the recordings was not the best. These have been stored in a garage since the 80's where the temperature ranged from very hot to extreme cold. There is one part of a recording that I think about often. The band is playing a familiar song and you can hear the crowd singing along in the background enjoying themselves. All of a sudden, you clearly hear someone break the balls at a pool table. I often try to imagine the scenery of that moment. I was most likely playing some video game or pinball machine. Those were the days that I wish I could return to. Not a care in the word and the entire bar having so much fun.

A few years ago, Dad went in for cataract surgery. They saw something they didn't like and did some scans. A couple days later, he was transferred from the V.A. directly into hospice. He had cancer in his brain. They had asked him if he wanted to do Chemo but after experiencing how it affected my brother. He decided it was best to let nature take its course.

I remember clearly the first time we came to visit him at the care center. When locating his room, we were told to go down a hallway. I thought they told us wrong because the sign said short term care. He wouldn't be leaving anytime soon, I thought. Then it hit me why he was in this section. Things were happening so quickly that I didn't process the immediacy of the situation. My mother stayed at our house during this time. I would drop her off at the care center on my way to work and we would come get her and visit with Dad in the evenings.

Robin and I had been planning a Raincheck Reception for a few months. We got married alone in Eureka Springs AR, and never had the experience of a wedding reception so we planned a party for our 20th anniversary. The party was a few weeks into Dad's stay at the care center. He made it to the reception, but it was obvious he wasn't doing great. At one point, he didn't know who I was for a few seconds. The next night, we came to pick up Mom from his room. Mom was feeding him which I thought was strange. He went to bed soon after. I said "bye", he responded "goodbye". We basically said the same word, but they had very different meanings. He died soon after we left that night.

Seward Polka Dotts was a beer drinking band. They didn't get paid a lot for shows but the beer was always on the house. The bars always made sure their cups were full. I remember one night after we got home Dad decided to get a drink out of the pantry for a shot. I was in the other room at the time, but I heard him say "This Vodka is as weak as water".

I really took his music talent for granted. I wish I could have a conversation today with him about the songs he played and sang. I have so many questions. I'm much more into his music now that he's gone than I was before. The same goes for our Czech heritage. We ate a lot of Kolaches over the years. It was a staple for every family gathering my entire life. This family recipe came directly from my cousin Adella Schulz who wrote Undocumented – A Young Man's Quest for the American Dream that tells the story of my great grandfather.

KOLACHE

INGREDIENTS
- ½ cup warm water
- 2 pkg. dry yeast
- 1½ cup lukewarm nonfat purified milk
- 2/3 cup sugar
- 2 tsp. salt
- ½ cub real butter
- 5 to 6 cups sifted flour

DIRECTIONS
1. Place warm (not hot) water in a bowl and sprinkle dry yeast over. Sprinkle approximately 1 teaspoon of sugar over yeast and blend. Let set until ready to use.
2. Combine milk, sugar, salt, and butter in a bowl; heat in microwave until lukewarm (not necessary to scald). Sift 1 to 2 cups of flour into milk mixture, beating continuously with electric mixer. When pasty, add yeast, which has been dissolved. Continue to add flour while sifting and beating until mixture will not carry. Continue to add flour, stirring with a wooden spoon until it is stiff enough to handle, but not as stiff as it should be for bread.
3. Cover and let rise until double in bulk. Always punch down using sifted flour while working with hands. Add small amounts of flour if dough is too runny. Let it rise again until doubled and ready to make into kolaches.

4. When the dough is ready to work, shape into bunlike amounts and place onto a well buttered black or aluminum baking pan. Then, brush with melted butter. Allow to rise a while. When it has risen, use your index finger to make a small indentation in the dough, but do not puncture the bottom. Fill each bun with a desired filling.
5. Bake in 375 degrees oven for the first 10-15 minutes. Continue to make at 350 degrees until golden brown. Brush again with melted butter. Remove from pan while slightly warm so they don't stick. Dust with powdered sugar before serving.

FRUIT-FILLING FOR KOLACHE

Any of the following:
- Fresh rhubarb
- Fresh Italian prunes
- Fresh Cherries

*Not as good as fresh but you can also use the "Solo" brand fruit that comes in cans.

POPPY SEED FILLING

INGREDIENTS
- 2 cups poppy seed
- 4 whole eggs
- 2 cups sugar
- Plumbed raisins (optional)

DIRECTIONS
1. Soak poppy seed in cold water overnight. In the morning, drain off water using a fine strainer.
2. Grind the seeds
3. Add sugar, and raisins; mix well.

COTTAGE CHEESE FILLING

INGREDIENTS
- ½ lb. dry cottage cheese
- ¾ cup sugar
- 2 tablespoons of flour
- 2 egg yolks
- ½ teaspoon of vanilla
- Plumbed white raisins (optional)

DIRECTIONS
1. Combine all ingredients and stir well.

CHICKEN CAKE

We found this recipe written in Dad's handwriting in his dresser drawer when cleaning out his room.

- 1 Tender Chicken
- 2 Legs
- 2 Breasts
- 1 Banana
- 3 Nuts
- 1 Cherry

DIRECTIONS

1. Take the tender chicken in your arms and two hand full of the breast and hold gently.
2. Take two legs spread apart.
3. Drop in banana and stir until good and hard.
4. Increase motion until good and hot.
5. Increase motion until banana creams, cherry pops.
6. Let cake cool. If cake rises, leave town.

Wood Fired Pizza is my greatest hit. It's what most people talk about and request. It was so popular at my house that my friends convinced me to start a food truck selling it. I had so much fun creating the recipes and giving them names. Here are some quotes from people over the years about my Pizza.

"I just wanted to let you know that I can honestly say that was the BEST pizza I have ever had!"

"The BBQ was my favorite. The sauce was the pathway of goodness from the crust to the burnt ends."

"Crusty dough...tantalizing ingredients...my mouth is watering now!"

"This is amazing, I kind of want to kiss you."

"The burnt ends Pizza is to die for, but I think the most pleasant surprise was the Thai Chicken. So delicious and unexpected. A mouth full of deliciousness! "

"This is the best pizza I've ever had, and I've been eating pizza for 80 years."

"You have ruined all other pizzas for me, forever! You better start delivering!"

JUNKSTOCK

Junkstock is a large festival-like atmosphere where antique dealers from across the region set up shops at an old farm right outside Omaha. They also had live music from local musicians all weekend and of course a handful of the best food trucks from the area. This happened to be the first gig I booked for Smoke-N-Pizza. It ran from Friday to Sunday. The fee to have a space there was $400. When I called inquiring, I said that we did BBQ and Pizza. They didn't have a pizza vendor yet and thought this would be a good addition. I don't recall telling them that we had never done this before. Fake it until you make it? We quickly learned that we needed to have insurance and also all of the rules of the truck. Water had to be a certain degree and we had to have a way to wash dishes, and refrigeration. The health inspector would be checking us before we could serve food that Friday morning.

I had been thinking about how I would run a restaurant of my own for years. Sometimes, it was the little things that I put a lot of thought into. We mounted speakers on the outside of our trailer so that we could have music playing to set the tone while customers were in line. I put together a mix tape of Robert Johnson and Muddy Waters. I was not that familiar with these two initially but when searching for the 'sound', they were it. Very old school Blues from the 30's-40's. I've heard similar music in really good BBQ restaurants in Kansas City. I also mixed in some traditional old Italian music. Instrumentals that included accordions. I spent hours selecting what I thought was the perfect playlist.

I also thought about the menu a lot. When we were getting ready to start this food truck venture, my brother was battling cancer. He had reached stage 4 and had decided to stop with chemo and radiation and move toward comfort care. We visited him as much as possible at the care center. He was interested in what I was doing, so I talked to him a lot about what foods we were going to sell and about the mobile wood fired pizza oven we were buying. At some point during this, we thought about dedicating a sandwich in his name. It would be smoked brisket on a unique bun made fresh at a bakery in Omaha. Our signature sandwich would be called "The Leslie". I hope that he was honored. We sold hundreds of them.

I mentioned the local bakery. We have been going there for years on Saturdays buying breads, buns, pizza dough, and whatever else looked good. The place is called Rotella's. There is always a large line and you have to pay cash. I contacted them because we wanted to have a good bun for our Leslie sandwich. I'm not sure why but the vice president took a liking to our story and invited us on a tour of their operations. He came up with a special bun that would be unique to just us and gave us a great deal on that plus pizza dough. This was really an exciting time of my life organizing all of this.

The menu for Junkstock was the Leslie sandwich, Brisket pizza, Thai chicken pizza, Buffalo chicken pizza, BBQ chicken pizza, pepperoni pizza, and cheese pizza.

I contacted the owner of Grandma Foster's BBQ sauce asking about buying in bulk. He also liked our story and I was buying gallon bottles and picking them up from his house at a large discount. We used the sauce on our pizza's and also had them outside our trailer for folks to add to their sandwiches if they wanted. We were sure to take the stickers off the containers so that our secret was kept safe.

When we arrived at Junkstock and got our spot, we quickly learned that there is a food vendors code of conduct. The vendor next to us asked us how much we were charging for soda and water. Everyone had to charge the same amount so that it was be fair. We were told that water was $3 a bottle. I had just bought several cases at Costco the night before for .18 apiece. The markup was insane!

I had smoked 2 large briskets and processed them into pieces the day before and stored them in large freezer bags. We had a small freezer in the trailer where we stored chicken, brisket, and pizza crusts. That weekend, we sold individual sized pizzas for $8. We funded the cash register with $500 in various bills and change. We were in pretty deep with costs before even opening.

There was a large roaster where we kept the brisket hot. I would add a couple cans of Campbell's double condensed beef broth along with a couple freezer bags of the brisket on 200 degrees and sprinkle in some Ed Rub. I referred to the rub as candy. It really made a difference to the taste. Once the roaster warmed up, you could smell the smoky flavor outside and it drew folks to the truck.

We were about to open when my wife, who was going to be the order taker went to our car to grab something quick. I was chopping vegetables getting my station ready and looked up to see someone standing at our window. He asked if he could have a pizza. My partner who cooked the pizzas gave me a nod stating the he was ready so I took his order. The cash register wasn't out yet so I put his money off to the side. Within a few minutes, the same thing happened over and over. By the time my wife got back to us, there were a few hundred dollars just sitting in a messy pile on our table. It was a good thing she was back because we now had a line.

I would listen to people as they ordered and made the pizza's quickly. Fortunately, it only took one minute to cook these small pizza's in our oven that we kept the temperature at 900 degrees.

There was a line of at least 25 people all day long. At one point, I went outside to cook pizza's for a while. There was a lady sitting next to where I was. She said to me "This is the best pizza I've ever had. And I've been eating pizza for 80 years!". I had been making these pizza's for friends and family for a while, but this was the first day I had cooked for people I didn't know. One of our favorite things to do is to watch people take the first bite of whatever they ordered. It seemed they were surprised on how good it tasted. This was validation for our hard work.

We had family come visit us that first day which was a relief because a couple hours in we ran out of cheese. They were kind enough to go buy more for us. By 2pm, we were completely sold out of food. We had to close down for the day. Our calculation was way off, we still had two more days to serve food. We cleaned up and counted the money. In addition to what we started with, there was $3,000 cash in the drawer. I think this was one of the happiest moments in my career. We only had a few hundred dollars in material. We were onto something special!

Back to reality! We had to be open to serve food the next mid-morning, so we went directly to Costco and bought another 6 large briskets along with more chicken and cheese. Fortunately, we had extra pizza crusts in my freezer at home. I was tired from standing and the fast pace of the day but there was no choice but to start a fire and start smoking the meat. This was a 12-hour process, so I tried to sleep an hour at a time so that I could check the fire and make sure the temperature was where it needed to be. After it was done cooking, it still needed to be processed. I didn't get much rest, but it was worth it and I still had energy since I was super excited about how the weekend was going.

I didn't think about the fact that most folks work Friday's and that Saturday would be even more busy. Same story as Friday but even more busy. We ran out of cheese, again. We ran out of chicken, and brisket, again. At one point, I was posting photos of our line and food on our FB page and noticed a post from our neighbor two trucks down. It was a photo of Mike and Frank from American Picker's. They were in the truck making a burger and eating. I'm a huge fan of the show and of course they would be here since Junkstock is a picker's dream. They didn't make it down to us. I wish that they did, that would have really been cool just to see them.

We ran out of food again and did the same prep for Sunday. The entire weekend was a blast and the organizers of Junkstock fell in love with us and invited us back for their next festival.

SMOKED BRISKET PIZZA

Sauce: BBQ (Grandma Fosters preferred)

Topping: Smoked Brisket

Cheese: Mozzarella and Muenster

If it's a small crowd, I make homemade dough. I've also bought frozen dough from our local bakery. When we have large parties and when we were doing the food truck, I would but frozen pre-made crusts from the local supermarket by the case. Do whatever is convenient to you. Thin crust has always been the crowd favorite way to go.

Put a small amount of BBQ Sauce on top of the crust and spread all the way to the edges. Put shredded mozzarella cheese on top covering all of the sauce completely. Next, top with smoked brisket. It can be chopped or even burnt ends. If you do not have brisket on hand, it's ok to buy it from your local BBQ place. I did this when I was experimenting with the brisket pizza early on. Finally use a bottle with a nozzle to drizzle sauce on top of the pizza. Making sure that you get it on as much of the brisket as you can. This will hopefully crystalize on top of the meat making it burnt end-like. Put a small amount of Muenster cheese, sliced or shredded on top.

I realize most folks don't have wood fired ovens, but you can get good results from the oven inside your house. The key is to get it very hot. 500 degrees is the best, in this case . These pizzas will cook fast so keep an eye on them. If you have a pizza stone, use it to make the crust extra crispy.

INTROVERTED

Hi! My name is Makala Neal. In 2006 I began a job that held a corporate office. At this corporate office there was a computer tech guy that would come and work on the computers at the stores I was associated with. This guy was very quiet when he would come to the stores. He would do his job on the computer and leave. He wasn't much for conversation, much less small talk. Sadly for him, this made me want to do it more. I would come up with all kinds of questions to ask him. After the first initial question, he would give me this look like 'Do we really have to go through this again today.' I think he finally realized that I wasn't going away and just gave into my offer of friendship. After a couple years I moved into the office where he worked. Daily he heard, "DAMNIT EDDIE!!" because something went wrong with my computer. He also heard "Mrrrr.. EEEDDDIIEEE!!" just to annoy him a tad. I would yell this from my desk so he could hear me just to make it more fun. He, as you know, was in a glass cubical strategically placed in the center of the room. After all the years this guy wasn't just a Help Desk guy to me, he became a great friend, even my best friend. This computer guy was Eddie Lance. (I'm sure you guessed that by now.)

Over the years Eddie, Robin and their family have become one of my own. We have been on many ventures together. Many he talks about in this book. From couples' trips, to the Pizza Wagon with Smoke N Pizza, a couple different bands, 1 wedding and 2 children (mine and my husband's of course!) MANY different instruments, a couple books, a T-shirt brand, raincheck receptions, tesla concerts, lots of computer questions, and many food recipes.... The list could go on and on! I have met so many great people through this couple including extended family members of theirs, friends like Jesse Curtis of Curtis Farms (who, I now consider a great friend of ours too) and the band members of Tesla, just to name a few.

Eddie and I have discussed many recipes. Knowing how great he is at creating things, I often love to come up with new challenges for him to make. After having much success with the famous BBQ Brisket Pizza, we decided to expand the sauce selection. The next one had to be something that would stand out and be as memorable as the first. Eddie and I had discussed this and had the idea of going in an interesting direction. This sauce was a thicker, sweeter sauce. Not something you would commonly find on a pizza. However, he liked experimenting, so we decided to give it a try. The type of sauce was something like I had tried somewhere, so he did a recreation of what he thought it would be. The sauce is named Captain Jack Whiskey Sauce. It has become a staple at their home parties. It pairs perfectly with the brisket and chicken pizza called Whiskey Brisket and Whiskey Chicken Pizza. Definitely a crowd pleaser.

WHISKEY BRISKET PIZZA

Sauce: Captain Jack Whiskey Sauce

Topping: Smoked Brisket

Cheese: Mozzarella

This is made the same way as the Smoked Brisket Pizza except without the Muenster cheese. The Whiskey sauce is sticky and is much thicker than the BBQ sauce, so you'll want to use a spoon to spread it out.

"It's the most amazing pizza I've ever eaten! Hands down!"

CAPTAIN JACK WHISKEY SAUCE

INGREDIENTS
- 11/3 cup dark brown sugar
- 1 head of garlic (roasted)
- 1 tablespoon of olive oil
- 3 tablespoons of minced white onion
- 2/3 cup of water
- 1 cup of pineapple juice
- 1/4 cup of teriyaki sauce (store bought)
- 1 tablespoon of soy sauce
- 3 tablespoon of fresh lemon juice
- 1 tablespoon of Honey Jack Whiskey (or any whiskey)
- 1 tablespoon of crushed pineapple
- ¼ teaspoon of ground cayenne pepper

DIRECTIONS
1. Wrap garlic in foil. Roast garlic in the oven for 45 minutes.
2. Combine all wet ingredients in a stove pot and start to boil. Add in all other ingredients. Leave on high until sauce reduces in half. Should be a syrup type consistency.

BUFFALO CHICKEN PIZZA

Sauce: Buffalo, Ranch

Topping: Cubed Chicken Breast

Cheese: Mozzarella

Using a spoon, spread buffalo sauce on pizza crust all the way to edges. Add chicken. Chicken can be cooked in oven, grilled, or slow cooked in a crockpot. Season with salt and pepper. You can use smoked chicken if you want. I found out it took away from the buffalo flavor we desired with this pizza.

Top with mozzarella cheese. I like to put sauce in a squeeze bottle and make a circle design on top. I also use spay butter on top of everything. This gives a nice yellow-orange finish when it cooks.

When pizza is done, you can optionally use a squeeze bottle to add ranch dressing on top, making a pretty design.

BUFFALO SAUCE

INGREDIENTS
- 23-ounce bottle of Frank's RedHot original sauce
- ½ stick of butter (unsalted)
- 3-4 cloves of garlic

DIRECTIONS
1. In a saucepan, simmer RedHot sauce and butter.
2. Mince garlic and add to saucepan.
3. Cook for 15 minutes and let cool.

THAI CHICKEN PIZZA

Sauce: Sweet Chili Sauce

Topping: Chicken, Cilantro, Red Bell Pepper, Carrot, Jalapeno, Sprouts.

Cheese: Mozzarella

Chop peppers and carrots however you like. I like to use a potato peeler on carrots to make really thin slices.

I've found that all sweet chili sauce is about the same so pick up whichever brand you want to. Spread sauce to the edges of crust. Add chicken. Chicken can be cooked in oven, grilled, or slow cooked in a crockpot. Season with salt and pepper. You can use smoked chicken if you want, I don't feel it is necessary. Add mozzarella cheese. Top with all vegetables except cilantro and sprouts. Cook pizza. The vegetables are not meant to be fully cooked when pizza comes out. Should be fresh and have a crispy crunch. Now add cilantro and sprouts and drizzle more chili sauce on top.

BBQ CHICKEN PIZZA

Sauce: Grandma Fosters BBQ Sauce

Topping: Chicken, Red Onion, Jalapeno, cilantro

Cheese: Mozzarella

Spread sauce to the edges of crust. Add chicken. Chicken can be cooked in oven, grilled, or slow cooked in a crockpot. Season with salt and pepper. You can use smoked chicken if you want, I don't feel it to be necessary.

Add mozzarella cheese.

Top with red onion and sliced or diced jalapeno.

Finally use a bottle with a nozzle to drizzle sauce on top of the pizza making a circular design.

Cook pizza. Before serving, add in chopped cilantro.

NOTHING BUT A GOOD PRIME

The music video for Poison's hit song "Nothin' But A Good Time," opens with a teenage boy working in the kitchen of a restaurant washing piles on piles of dirty dishes. This was pretty much my life in 1989. The servers would drop by my cleaning station with trays full of dirty plates and grimy silverware for me to make clean by hand. There was rarely any downtime with this gig, because no matter how quickly I cleaned one plate, a waiter would come back with two more. Listening to Poison on the radio helped me through even the most mind-numbing of evenings. Head over to YouTube and watch the video to get a visual representation of my weekend work shifts.

Fast forward 28-years-later, my wife Robin, Frank Hannon, and I were walking down a long empty hallway backstage at a Def Leppard concert. All the sudden, as if we opened that kitchen door in the music video, Bret Michaels from Poison suddenly appeared at the other end of the hallway and he was walking towards us. In the late 80's, Poison was my favorite band and I had seen them countless times, both in my teen and adult life, but I had never met anyone in the band in real life. As he came closer, it dawned on me what was about to happen.

Frank and Bret are good friends, their bands were touring together at the time, and they had toured together many other times before then, especially early in their careers. In fact, I was first introduced to Tesla's music while attending a Poison show back in 1989 where they were the opening act.

"Hey Bret, these are my good friends Robin and Eddie!"

Bret reached out to shake my hand, I was completely starstruck. Almost 30-years-later and he looked just like I remembered from old Metal Edge magazines from back in the day. He was decked out in his trademark bandana and his own merch. I was so in awe of what was happening I don't even remember what or if I said anything.

"Eddie actually is the person who started the website that helped us get back together," Frank told him.

"What! No way, that's awesome! The internet is crazy right?" Bret responded as he reached out to shake my hand again enthusiastically. "It's so nice to meet you!"

"It's nice to meet you too, Bret Michaels," I responded as I was trying to contain myself.

Frank and Bret started small talking for a bit, but I have no memory of what they were saying. I was recovering from what Bret had just said to me. We eventually said our goodbyes, Bret shook my hand for a 3rd time, and we all parted ways. As we returned to walking down the hallway, Frank started singing,

"Every rose has its thorn! Just like every night has its dawn!"

On the other end of the hallway, we heard Bret finish the chorus for Frank,

"Just like every cowboy sings a sad sad song! Every rose has its thorn!"

One of the most surreal moments ever.

The following recipe is for Prime Rib, just how I used to make it in High School at the Dandy Lion Inn.

DANDY LION PRIME RIB

INGREDIENTS

- 1 ten-pound rib roast
- Garlic salt
- Pepper

DIRECTIONS

1. Generously rub spices all around roast.
2. Preheat oven to 500 degrees
3. Bake for 20 minutes
4. Reduce heat to 375 and bake for additional 75 minutes.
5. You can also smoke at 200 degrees for 2 hours first and then finish in oven on 375 for 60 minutes or until it's done to your preference. Below is a guideline to help.

INTERNAL TEMPERATURE

Rare: 120-125 degrees

Medium Rare: 130-135 degrees

Medium: 135-140 degrees

Medium Well: 140-145 degrees

Well Done: 145 degrees or higher

BACKSTAGE PASS

BE CAREFUL WHAT YOU WISH FOR

I always have my cell phone with me. It's not far from the bed when I sleep because I often get support calls in the middle of the night from work. This night seemed like all the others. The phone rang at 2AM. I picked up the phone and the caller ID read "Mom". My mother was living at a care center at the time and always went to bed by 8pm. This was not logical. I handed the phone to Robin because I was still trying to process what was going on.

"I can't find the kids, where are they?" Mom said. You could hear she was clearly upset by the tone of her voice.

"Mom, the kids are here in bed. Everything is fine". Robin replied.

"No, I just put them to bed and now I can't find them!" Mother continued in a panic.

"I think you were having a dream, Mom. They are here safe with us in Omaha".

The next day, we were to have a birthday party at the care center for her, but we had decided to cancel it. The immediate family was all still going to be there though. In my mind as I was driving us to Lincoln, I had the most awful thought. "Please can this just be over?" My mom had a difficult time later in life with a couple heart attacks. More recently, she had lost her husband and two sons. She had pretty much given up long ago. I guess I had given up on her too. The conversations for the past year had all been similar. She'd ask me if I talked to Tesla and ask what I had been cooking. More recently she would ask me the same question within 20 minutes. I thought "Are you fucking with me, Mom?" in my head. "She just asked that, what is going on?"

We got to the care center and visited with her. Soon after, things started getting strange. I'd notice that she would look off to the side and smile as if she was acknowledging someone. She'd say, "Come on in". The problem was there was nobody there. We ended up shutting all the doors because it got a little creepy. We'd laugh about it though because what else were you supposed to do?

"Mother, there is nobody there."

When I was hugging her and saying goodbye, she pointed out the window and said quietly

"Your friends are out there waiting for you."

That would have been a nice surprise, but it was not true. She was taken to the ER not long after we left. A couple of days later, we were all there by her side as she passed away.

That was it. Mom was always the main cook when it came to holiday get togethers. I learned a lot by just watching her make meals. I wish that I had asked more questions. Here is the recipe for what she was famous for in our family.

Thank you to my sister Linda for the recipe.

MOM'S APPLE PIE

INGREDIENTS
- 9 X 13 pan

Crust
- 2 cups flour
- 2/3 cup Crisco shortening
- 2/3 cup water

DIRECTIONS
1. Mix with a fork. Divide in half and wrap each half in wax paper. Place in refrigerator.
2. 10-12 large Granny Smith's Apples
3. Peel and quarter apples and place in large bowl with ice water and a little lemon juice.
4. Roll out one of the crusts and place in bottom of pan.
5. Slice apples into a new bowl and add
   - 2 cups sugar
   - 1/2 cup flour
   - 3 tablespoons cinnamon
6. Mix thoroughly and place on top of bottom crust in pan.
7. Roll out top crust and place in top of apple mixture.
8. Sprinkle top crust with
   - 2/3 cup sugar
   - 2 teaspoons cinnamon

9. Prick top crust several times with a fork.
10. Bake on cookie sheet to help with overflow while cooking.
11. Bake at 450 degrees for 15 minutes
12. Turn down to 350 degrees and bake for an additional 45- 60 minutes.

JENNA REESE LANCE

My dad and I have bonded through music and his creative recipes over the years. My mom worked night shifts when I was in kindergarten-2nd grade, which meant that he was left to come up with stuff to keep me busy in the evenings. We drove around a lot together, where he would put in local indie rock band albums in the cd player. Our favorites were Bright Eyes, Neva Dinova (Jake Bellows), and The Good Life. Those are still my favorite bands today. We most often went around thrift store to thrift store looking for Furbies for my collection, and miniature keyboards and reel-to-reel players for his collection. It was so much fun to look around and sometimes hit the jackpot with a new find.

I remember one night we went to a local record store to buy a new CD, "The Album of the Year" by The Good Life. The cashier told us he was the drummer for the band! That is super cool looking back on since the band gained popularity. Our next stop of that night was to drive around to different Hy-Vees (a Midwest exclusive grocery store) to sample cheeses at the deli and decide what would be perfect for my dad's soon-to-be "Sweet Sandwiches". We learned what Havarti was that night and thought it was the most amazing thing!

We always ended up having little fun adventures together, regardless whatever life threw our way. Life hasn't been all good to my family, but I feel that through experiencing loss and difficulty early on has made me into an empathetic person that can make light and find humor during bad situations. I remember around 2011 my dad lost his job. During those months, I never once saw him demotivated. He constantly worked by applying for jobs, cooking, and flipping thrift-store and garage-sale finds on EBay. I remember being home with him during this time where we would watch The Talk, The Chew, and have Food Network on even when those shows weren't playing. Sometimes, the recipes inspired us, but other times we laughed and pointed out when the T.V. chefs were trying too hard.

Early on in my childhood, I decided I didn't want to eat meat anymore. Knowing of my dad's classic recipes, you might think that this could've upset him- but he fully supported my decision. I think that this excited him and pushed him into trying out new recipes. Every single meal we cooked from then on out accommodated me. To this day he still thinks of unique recipes for me. My favorite dish he makes is "All in the Pool Pasta". It has all my favorite ingredients just like all the crazy adventures we have had together.

SWEET SANDWICHES

INGREDIENTS

- Tomato, sliced thin
- Small Red Onion, sliced thin
- Lettuce, shredded
- Banana Pepper Rings from jar
- Red Wine Vinegar
- Extra Virgin Olive Oil
- Salt, Pepper, Red Pepper Flakes, Garlic Powder, Onion Powder, Oregano
- Havarti Cheese Slices
- Provolone Cheese Slices
- Pepperoni, Ham, Salami
- Soft French Bread loaf cut in half.

DIRECTIONS

1. Assemble sandwich with meat, cheese, tomato, pepper, onion.
2. The key to this sandwich is the "Sweet" sauce (not sweet as in sugary but sweet as in "Right On!"). Combine equal amounts of vinegar and EVOO. Add in dashes of dry seasoning. Toss lettuce in sauce and pour on top of sandwich. Go ahead and pour additional sauce on top for more sweetness. Cut sandwich into slices and serve.
3. You can use the lettuce and sweet sauce mixture to make a Sweet Salad. Add a generous amount of dried parmesan cheese on top of salad and serve.

ALL IN THE POOL PASTA

INGREDIENTS
- 1 Box Penne Pasta cooked al dente
- 1 fresh package of Spinach, chopped
- 1 Jar of Artichokes, chopped
- 1 Pint Cherry Tomatoes all cut in half
- 4 tablespoons chopped white onion
- 4 tablespoons chopped garlic
- 1 tablespoon oregano
- 1tsp. basil
- 1 teaspoon of red pepper flakes
- Salt and pepper to taste
- Dried Parmesan Cheese
- Mozzarella Cheese, shredded
- ½ stick non salted butter
- ¼ cup extra virgin olive oil

DIRECTIONS
1. Sautee onion and garlic in butter for several minutes before adding in spinach, artichokes, and tomatoes. Add in EVOO and continue to cook on low for 10 minutes while adding in all other dry seasoning.
2. Add mixture to pasta while adding in ¼ cup of dry parmesan cheese. Mix together and transfer to cooking dish. Sprinkle mozzarella cheese on top and take on 450 degrees until cheese is golden brown.

WAY BACK HOME

Last year, I returned to my hometown of Staplehurst to record footage for a music video the song "Home", my band had just recorded. As I drove into town past the Big Blue River, I didn't see any prospectors. Honestly, I don't think many (if any) locals know about the missing gold. I learned about it from a missing treasure book I stumbled upon some years ago. I imagine that after this book comes out there may be a slight increase in metal detector activity in the area though. We have done a little hunting ourselves since I learned of this story. No bait purses in the road either as I drove into town. The kids must be playing more modern games these days.

I drove around town filming the main street from my car on an old camcorder. After I finished the shoot, I went over to the single standing bar in town for lunch. This is where I played pinball, Pac-man, dig dug, and pool for the first time a lifetime ago.

After lunch, I decided to step outside for some fresh air. I walked across the street to the old park where my childhood friends and I spent so much time hanging out. I sat on one of the old swings and looked towards the empty plot of land where the Sport Tavern once stood. It had burned down years before. To the left is the house I grew up in was still standing. An unkept lawn had the front door completely covered in bushes. The pink paint that Dad put on when we moved there was almost all peeled off. If that house was not haunted when I lived there it certainly is now.

A lot of the same playground equipment was still in the park. The worn jungle gym in front of me was added in the mid 70's. My good friend Tony, the son of my mentor Scott and I were on the front page of the local newspaper sitting on it the week they put it in. The entire town was just a shell of what it once was.

Suddenly out of nowhere A beautiful Monarch butterfly flew towards me. It looked so pretty and full of life, so I put my arm out and it landed on me. It stayed in place for a little while before it began hovering right in front of my eyes, obstructing my vision. It looked like it was trying to tell me something. I felt peace come over me, I knew it had been sent to comfort me. It sensed my relief and flew off. Hopefully, it will tell its buddies to visit me as well.

An exaggerated truth about how I met my favorite band

"Order up!"

"Got it." Penny said, taking the Chicken Fried Steak Dinner off the counter.

"Thank you!" I said. "Are there any customers?"

"Not right now." she said.

"Cool, I'll be washing dishes, then. Let me know if you need me."

"Sure thing." she said, moving away towards the dining room as I moved towards the kitchen.

And that's how it was in the summer of '92. To be honest, it was a cool gig. Cooking, washing, generally hanging out at the Dandy Lion Inn; you couldn't ever really say the place was busy, and cooking a few steaks or chicken every hour was alright by me. I had no complaints, and it was great saving for the bills that I was sure I'd be having once I left in the fall and enrolled in college.

"Hey loser, pass the dish soap."

Oh. And Jesse.

"Here. Don't use it all in one place." I said passing him the soap.

Jesse and I had been friends since before I could remember. Getting the job here with him had been a huge plus to the whole thing, and even on the most awful days we had fun together.

Life was good. But on that day, it was about to get better.

Now when I washed dishes, I never did it just to the sound of the faucet; I always had a radio on in the background, jamming out to some tunes. I flipped the radio on, like I always did, and we rocked out to Nirvana and the Chili Peppers as we washed the dishes.

That night, however, a commercial came on the radio that caught our attention:

Atlanta sold out in 10 minutes. Kansas City in 5. How long will it take you Omaha?

EDISON! The Grand Ball Tour. September 19th Omaha Civic Auditorium.

Tickets go on sale tomorrow morning at all ticket stop locations.

"Holy shit." Jesse said. I nodded. "*Edison* is coming to Omaha?"

"Yeah." I said. "And they sold out in 10 minutes in other places."

"Are you thinking what I'm thinking?" Jesse said. I nodded again. I was doing a lot of nodding that night.

"Let's get the hell out of here." I said. "If we're quick, we can make it there before midnight and camp out for the tickets."

Anxious to get out of the kitchen, we started a major clean-up early. The restaurant closed at 10:00pm. It was currently 9:15pm but we hadn't had a single order for a good hour. So, I left the grill and fryers on but put everything else away and started cleaning up. I convinced Jesse to do the mopping while I chatted with the hostess up front. Right as I took my apron off at 9:55, the only waitress left that night rang the bell. It was an order of 3-piece chicken. Wonderful, it takes a full 15 minutes to deep fat fry chicken and I had already ditched the egg wash and flour mixture. I looked over at the trash where Jesse had recently disposed the extra cooked chicken, we had on hand from earlier that night. I counted the pieces in my head. Then I rationed it out, trying to convince myself what was I was about to do was ok. It was sitting on top of a few sheets of clean paper towels. Could I dig it out and re-fry it for a few minutes?

Jesse and I clocked out at 10:05pm and headed towards Lincoln to start our up all night adventure.

What? Don't judge me! I was only 17 years old. Besides that, the week following we started a new special due to the customer comments. Twice fried chicken I called it; it was a huge success and continued for years after I left for college. The only modification was that we stored the first run frying chicken in a big, clean white bucket covered, and refrigerated it.

I turned my ball cap backwards and lit a cigarette before getting in my 1980 AMC Spirit. Jesse rode shotgun and we were on our way.

We stopped at another buddy's apartment where we picked up a couple other folks that wanted to get in on those tickets. All the buzz at his pad was Vince Neil's departure from *Motley Crew* that day. I knew Jesse was a huge crue-head, so I gave him crap all night saying, "Motley Who?"

"You'd better hope *Edison* never breaks up Freddy." Jesse said with a smirk.

"Don't even joke about that, Jesse!" I replied.

We all arrived at Ticket Stop around midnight. There wasn't any sort of line, so we headed over to the 24-hour diner a few blocks away to kill some time until they opened at 10:00am. Everyone ordered chicken except me and Jesse, who looked at each other with a knowing glance. We each ordered a soda.

Come 10:05am, we all had tickets in hand. The show did sell out, as we all knew it would. It took a little longer than we thought. It was more like 2 weeks instead of 2 minutes. Back then all shows were general admission, so we didn't benefit much from pulling the all-nighter. Except, you know, that it gave us a night we'll never forget. All these years later, it's still fresh in my mind.

We worked the day of the big show. Somehow, we managed to power through it, even though we both wanted to get out of there and head to Omaha. By the time night came, the world had taken on that fuzzy haze, you know? The one you can only get by not sleeping for a while, and we managed to sit through the opening band and not fall asleep.

Then, with all the lights still on, Hank came out and started playing his Gibson SG. It was like nothing I had ever seen before. Typically, the lights go out creating complete darkness before the band comes out. Not *Edison*, they just came out and started the show.

Everything melted away. The tiredness, the haze, everything; the adrenaline kicked in and we shot to our feet as the crowd roared, and we went from being in a stupor to being electrified with excitement. It wasn't a haze, it was something different:

it's that heightened sense of reality that you can only get at a concert, when time slows down, and everything becomes crystal clear. You can hear every note that comes out of the guitar, and the crash of the drums that beats in time with your heart. You become a part of the crowd, alone but united. You don't notice anything but the way you move, react, and feel with the music.

It's hard to describe. I guess you had to be there, you know?

And that's how the night went. If you want details, I'm sorry; I can't really give them to you. The whole night is a wild blur of sounds and sight, a Picasso of all my senses; I can only tell you how the silver gleam of their outfits melded with the scream of the guitars as my friends and I rocked out.

I remember the night vividly- well, I shouldn't say that. I feel the night vividly. Still do. And I remember going to sleep, and feeling so pumped: the best night of my life to date. I remember how that felt, and that's how Edison feels to me.

That night with Edison, well... that was a wild night. Like I said, I still remember it (feel it).

The good news is that I recovered from that night. Recovered well enough, in fact, that I got through college: I decided I'd go the programmer route, and I was fluent in all the drudgery of computer programming: C++, assembly language, integers, floats, pointers, blah blah and yadda yadda. Ready to join the real world.

Oh, and I also survived Edison breaking up.

Yeah, I said break up. It was a real big disappointment, you know? I heard about it on the radio; it happened close to the end of my junior year. They were getting bigger back then.

I called my buddies, Jesse and them, and they had heard about it too. I guess one of the guys had gotten too into his drugs, and the rest of the group called it quits when he couldn't even stagger to the stage to perform. It came as a shock to me, really; a shock to all of us. Edison to us wasn't a band, made up of men. It was a group, a kind of mix of light and sound that thundered down to us from atop its metal-and-wood throne. They were literally rockstars in every sense of the word.

But we got over it. At least, we said we did. It lingered with me for a while. I tried to tell myself it didn't matter, that all rock groups break up. And, I guess if you want the truth, I didn't think about it all that much, except when an Edison song came on the radio or I jammed out to them on the highway.

Jesse and the guys never mentioned it, and neither did I, but there it was: it lingered for me.

When I finally got out of college, I was a programmer, like I said: I didn't know anything about this new Internet, though. I wanted to learn some HTML, which is the programming language for the Internet. I got my hands on an HTML introduction book, and I thought about what kind of page to make.

A "Hello, World" page? Nah! Too corny. A page to say hi to my family? A news page? A page of stuff I was interested in?

None of it really grabbed me. I didn't want to make a website that had no interest to me, and for a while I put off even learning HTML.

And that was when I heard it: like a gunshot tearing through my consciousness, the opening chords of "The Grand Ball", Edison's, seared across the airwaves into my radio and out of the speakers.

And that's when I knew what site to make.

It was a simple site: I still have it archived, It looked so 90's, yet ahead of its time: it's had frames, and moving pictures, and just a few links to sites about Edison, along with an old MIIDI file that played fuzzy audio right at you from your computer speakers.

Most importantly, however, it had big, bold letters. Right on the front:

"OPERATION REUNITE EDISON"

I was so proud of it, when I finished. And, well... okay, yeah, I had a beer or two while I was making it. I put it up late on a Friday afternoon, and I decided to log off for the day and head out to the bar to keep the beers flowing.

Anyway, things happened, and for one reason or another I didn't ever get back to a computer that weekend to check it out.

Fast forward to Monday morning, I was reading up a bit more on HTML at home when I got a phone call.

"Hey bud. It's Mark." Mark said. "Something's up with your email."

"Up with my email? What do you mean?" I said.

"I Dunno. Every email I send you just gets bounced back as undeliverable." Mark said. "I thought I should let you know in case you were expecting anything important."

"Ah, damn." I said. "Alright, I'll go take a look, Thanks."

I got off the phone and walked over to my computer. I booted up, dialed in with my brand-spanking new 56k modem, and I hit my email button. I waited.

Nothing happened. I swore under my breath. I waited some more. Nothing happened. I swore a bit more. I reached for the phone to call my internet company.

And then something happened.

Thousands of emails popped up on my screen, along with an ominous message: "Mailbox full."

I grumbled. Someone had probably hacked my account, or I got spammed, or something. I resolved to go through my inbox and clear out all the spam emails, carefully saving whichever ones were actual emails and not spam.

I noticed something, though. Almost immediately. They all had titles like this:

"YEAH BRO GET EDISON BACK"

"oh my god you're so right! i love edison"

"I love Edison"

"EDISOOOOOOOOON"

You know, on and on. All in a weekend. All from my rinky-dinky site. And none of it was spam. I checked the website.

It was down. I cursed again, and I called my service provider.

"Excuse me," I said when I got someone on the line. "My site's down, and I'd like to know what happened."

"Sure thing." the man said. "Domain name?"

"edisonweb.com" I told him.

"Holy cow, you're edisonweb.com?" he said. "Sorry dude, it'll be down for a while. You got tens of thousands of hits in hours yesterday; it overwhelmed our servers. We're actually upgrading them now to handle the load."

"Oh, uh, ok." I said. "Thanks."

I hung up. And that's when I knew my mission for real.

It was time to bring Edison back.

The rest of it, well... honestly, it sounds more like some sort of movie than anything else.

I knew the website had a huge amount of oomph- anyone could see that, based on how it overwhelmed my web company's servers and all. People wanted them back.

But how was I going to get to them? The Internet wasn't really a big thing back then. Even a website with that many hits probably didn't even come close to a blip on Edison's radar. I needed a way to get in touch with them.

So, I did the obvious. I hacked into the editor of the leading Rock Magazine's email and got Ryan White's email address.

What? Don't judge me, I was still relatively young, and I was pumped. I got it through a little bit of con artistry, I started out by calling the receptionist. I looked on their web site- it was Joan, and their assistant editor's name was Jerry.

"Hey Joan!" I said cheerily when she picked up the phone. I thought of a fake name pretty quick. "It's Bill, how are you?"

"Hey Bill!" she said. "I'm fine, thanks. And you?"

"Good." I said. "Hey, listen; can you give me Jerry's number? I have a question about the Top 100 piece coming up and I can't find my address book. I think I lost it."

"Sure thing, Bill!" she said. "Just a second. It's 555-5438."

"Thanks!" I said. I hung up, and dialed the number she gave me. I started to sweat a little. It was now or never, all or nothing- here's how it all went down.

"Hello?" I heard a voice say.

"Hello. Is this Jerry?" I said, in as professional sounding voice as I could.

"This is he." Jerry said. "How can I help you?"

"This is Stuart, down in the computer room." I said. My palms were really starting to sweat now. "There's been some issues with wrong email addresses in our global mail servers, and I was told to get in touch with you to verify one of them."

"Uh, yeah, sure." James said. "Which one do you need?"

"Uh..." I said, pretending to flip through some papers. "A Mr. Ryan White. I have here rwhite@aol.com. Is that correct?"

"Nope, must be an old one." Jerry said. "He's rwhite123@aol.com now."

"Ah, alright." I said as nonchalantly as I could. "I'll be sure to update the mail servers then. I'll give you a ring back in a bit if we have any further problems. Thank you!"

"No problem." Jerry said. "Later."

I hung up, sweaty and nervous and still unbelieving. Holy shit. I did it.

Now that I had Ryan's personal email address, I could finally get to someone in the band and show them my intentions with the web site. With all the excitement concerning the new movement on the internet, I was anxious and a bit frightened at the same time. I sent him the email showing as much professionalism I could, knowing it was going to a member of my favorite band of all time. It took all I had in me not to build in lyric references of Edison's songs in my sentences. I thought it was clever but he's probably heard it all before. I simply said a quick hello and gave him the link to my web site.

The next morning, I connected to my modem and checked my mail. Buried in the middle of the 50 new messages of mostly Edison fans sending me well wishes was a reply from Ryan White himself. It read like a form letter.

Freddy,

Thank you for the e-mail. Enjoy the old Edison record's and move on with your life. Check out my new band Motorman. My address is below if you want to buy our new record for $10. Post that on your web site.

Ryan

Is he crazy? I just don't understand how a member of the best rock and roll band ever would not be into reforming and makin' magic again. What do I care about some other band he's in? How could it compare? I decided to give it a chance or at least keep on his good side and send him the ten bucks. I sent cash just to speed things up.

Two weeks later, I was still waiting for the CD to come in the mail so I decided to email him to ask what the holdup was. He responded a couple days later saying that he accidently burned my "check" in the fireplace and to send another one. Wait a minute, check? I didn't send a check. What is he trying to pull? I was a bit irate. I immediately sent him an email that opened the door for an anger moment for him as well.

Ryan,

You must be hard up for cigarette money to try to get me to pay you again for your stupid CD. I take it you didn't save all your Edison millions?

Freddy

A few minutes after hitting send on that email my phone rang. I have no idea how he got my number but there was a founding member of Edison on the other side of the phone screaming at the top of his lungs at me for me making such accusations in that email. I didn't have much of a chance to say anything as he was foaming at the mouth cursing me out. I had a million questions for him, why did they really break up, what does some lyric mean in one of their songs, and so on and so forth. He ended the conversation saying again that Edison will not be getting back together; he told me to check out the new projects, and to move on with my life.

I called my buddy directly after Ryan hung up on me.

"Dude, you won't believe who just called me." I said.

"Who? Must be someone important. You just screeched like a little girl."

"Ryan White, dude!" I said. "And I didn't screech."

"Woah!" Jesse said into the phone. "What did he call you for? Did he like the site? Holy shit!"

I told Jesse that he loved the site, and that he gave me some ideas on things I can expand on to make the site bigger. As I was lying to my buddy about how the conversation really went down, it dawned on me. Embrace the new bands to get close to the band.

Brilliant.

The next morning, I put a new widget on the top of Operation Reunite Edison. I wrote a script that did a calculation on how long the band had been broken up based on the current time and date. The header read:

"Edison has been broken up for 4 years, 6 month, 4 days, and 24 minutes. Move on with your life…"

Under that I posted some information about Ryan's new band and how to get their new CD.

The next morning, my sister called me saying she tried to email me but her message wouldn't go thru. She was getting some sort of mailbox full message. I quickly logged onto the internet to see what was up.

At this point, I was getting hundreds of new visitors each day and the newbies definitely did not get my sense of humor. This was my first experience of "hate mail". People telling me they grew up listening to Edison and that they will NOT move on with their lives. Funny, I was trying to make light of the situation and people took it the wrong way. Oh well, they will catch on soon. I started to reply to everyone as I normally did but after a while, I just clicked on the delete button over and over again.

A few days later, the Motorman CD arrived in the mail. It was much harder sounding than the Edison records but I did like it. So much in fact, that I dedicated a whole page on the web site for them. After some time, Ryan gave me a call and asked me to make an official web site for his band. I agreed and created my first "paid" web site. I also got on Ryan's mailing list. The first mass email he sent out promoting a show he was doing had a recipient that I was not expecting. Hank the guitarist from Edison. I couldn't believe Ryan had made the mistake of leaving that open for me to see. Now, I had an in on another member. I thought about it for a while and started composing an email to my guitar hero. Same old thing you know, I love all your work, do you think Edison will ever get back together? That sort of thing. A few days later, I got a response from Hank.

Right On Freddy!

I still love the music we made, it's not a matter of if we will get back together, it's when.

Check out my name band Southern Mayne. We're playing the Boardwalk in Sacramento on July 1st.

Rock on,

Hank

I immediately updated my web site with information on Hank's new band along with info on the Boardwalk show. I found out later that Ryan intentionally let me see Hank's email address so that I could get in touch with him. I guess Ryan isn't as bad as I had thought. I had a new respect for him.

It wasn't long before I was the webmaster for the official Southern Mayne web site. Both bands were not getting much attention in the rock magazines and MTV had stopped caring about music, so this was a difficult time to getting exposure. This is where the websites came into play. The internet was just starting to become mainstream and people were searching for info on Edison the band. Now both bands were touring the country in clubs and because of the web site exposure, people were coming to see them. The first chance I got to see Hank post-Edison was in Denver, Colorado opening for Judas Priest. This was the first time I was ever treated with special privileges as well. I was on the guest list and didn't have to pay anything to get it. On top of that, the band was so gracious to me and my posse. They were thanking me, hugging me, and giving me all sorts of keepsakes. I felt like the rock star that night. I had come a long way from that greasy kitchen in High School.

I would try to make some sort of update on the Operation Reunite Edison web site each day. What the guys were up to and if they happened to cover an Edison song the night before. I started to notice that from time to time the things that I typed would end up in the rock magazine's and occasionally local and national radio. All access passes to shows, free eats and drinks backstage, and lots of talk with the guys about their former band. Asking them each time I saw them if it was time to think about a reunion yet.

It started to get pretty crazy, believe it or not. The flood of visitors to the website was crazy. My web host had to upgrade twice more to accommodate all the new traffic. I'd get people coming up to me at shows, telling me all sorts of stuff about my site. They'd tell me how awesome it was, and how totally in they were on the whole idea, and they asked me for autographs and shit. It was absolutely insane.

One day I was sitting at work and my cell phone rings. I answered and the voice on the other end was Edison's lead singer.

"Hey Freddy. My name is Keith I was in a band called Edison."

"I know who you are." I replied.

Who wouldn't know with that recognizable voice? He could read the dictionary and I would buy a ticket to the show. He had heard from the grapevine what I was doing for the other bands and wanted me to help them out too. I was overwhelmed. Now, I'm doing 3 web sites for these guys' new projects. They did not even all talk to each other since the breakup. Yet, I was the link to all of them. Life was good.

It was really good, in fact. Some other big bands had heard about what I was doing for these guys, and I started my own website company that catered to some famous rock bands. I did sites for tons of guys: I can't name names, you know contracts and all that, but let's just say you've definitely heard of them. These are guys that sell out arenas, you know? Big time stars with big time personality.

Anyway, it was all good, but it got better, way better. One day, I got an email from Keith. I saved it. It was only a line, but it was the best damn line of email I've ever received in my life. It was freaking poetry. Here it is:

"Need your help. We're getting the band back together, need promo and news byte on website. Please call me. Thanks!"

And that's when it was on, baby! So on! I called Keith as fast as I could, and we hashed out the details for the promo as fast as we could. I got on the line with my graphic designer, and within two days I had a whole new design up with the Edison promo, and all the other websites linking to it.

"RECHARGED: EDISON LIVES AGAIN WORLD TOUR"

As you can imagine, the whole thing took off like a fighter jet. The website lit up, went down again, came back up. I got thousands of emails, phone calls, you name it: and all of them were saying the same things:

"OMG is this for real?"

"Holy shit dude you're my hero!"

"omg omg omg this is crazy"

and, you know, stuff like that. As the first day of the reunion tour neared, I was treated to one of the most epic experiences of my life: I got personally flown out to Sacramento to crash a few nights in Ryan White's mansion, and it was by far one of the best places I've ever stayed in my life.

For a young kid like me back then, it was amazing. It was everything you dreamed a rock star's mansion to look like. Huge hallways with priceless stuff, a recording studio in the basement, a huge pool and hot tub in the back.

Oh- and booze. Lots and lots of top-shelf stuff. I will say this: the nights leading up to the concert were some of the craziest and most awesome nights I've ever had in my life. I partied like a rock star, and damn, do they know how to live.

And then the day came. The first tour. I walked down into the dressing room with them, said good luck, and wandered out to the crowd. It was blinding and brilliant. The opening band was alright, nothing special. Then, I suddenly got a curious sense of Deja vu.

And then it hit me all over again.

The stage rumbled to life with the fireworks and flames that signaled Edison's triumphant return. The crowd screamed for them as their guitars screamed back and forth, excited to be back in the action. Every lick was the same, every pulse-pounding solo as good as they ever were, I was brought back to that night years ago, when I got swept away in the hazy mix of music, lights, and sound.

It was a damn good show. I met with the band afterwards, and I told them how amazing it was. They thanked me, and I left and went back on my way home.

I don't really believe that I was the reason Edison got back together. However, I was in the front row eating popcorn, and watching it all happen!

High School Reunion

A short story by Eddie Lance

"Why did you do it?!" someone yelled at me.

"They all deserve what they got. I have no regrets," I replied.

Everyone is always surprised when it happens in their town. They never expect it. They interviewed everyone: the mayor, schoolteachers, and even the gas station attendant that helped me just days prior to the incident. "I went to school with him. We used to sit next to each other on the bus and talk. He was always cracking' jokes," she said to a reporter.

Such uproar, because of me; the town wouldn't soon forget. Heck, I wouldn't want them to—I changed the lives of 5 families that day—forever.

People often told me I looked like the guy that would come into a building and shoot everyone in sight. Why couldn't have these same people instead told me that my shoes sure looked nice or that it was nice to see me that day? It wouldn't matter to me if they meant those words or not, because I could assume the best scenario. If someone says you look like an axe murderer, it's not likely they're saying it just to be kind, you know? Something had to be done. Timing would be the key, and everything came together brilliantly for me that night. People always say, "Let's see what tomorrow brings..." I decided the night prior that I was going to be what tomorrow brings—and I was...

It was the week of my 20th High School Reunion. I had no interest going to the 10th, but for some reason, this time, I really wanted to see everyone again. I got in my car and started to drive. I only had a little over an hour to get back home. I used the time to reflect on the memories that had been replaying in my head over and over again in my adult years.

I don't know if you've ever driven down a road through a place you haven't been in a while. It's a strange feeling, and your memory plays tricks on you. It's almost like a dream—you pass these places that you remember so well, that you swear you could reconstruct them brick by brick. When you see them, though, they're slightly different; they're old and worn, almost the same, but not quite.

I passed a ball field near the school as I drove. It was overgrown now, and all the clean-cut grass in the outfield had given way to thick weeds and underbrush after years of abandonment and disuse. Not for me, though—I remembered it the way it was, when I used to play football there after school. I could see myself and the other kids, lining up on a nice day, waiting to get picked for teams.

We would all race to the home plate of the ball field. The first two kids there were captains, and they took turns choosing players for their team. Being the last one picked was always pretty discomforting. See, the kid didn't really choose you—he had no choice—always an awkward moment for both the player and the captain. And no, I wasn't chosen last in this case, if you were wondering. I was 2nd to last.

The game we were playing was football. Our leader, Rocky, was really into the sport. He went on to play in college and made a pretty good name for himself, I guess, and now he's a local celebrity back home. He sells cars and is always on TV wearing his old jersey. At any rate, I was on his team the last day of school in 4th grade. There were no quarters when we played. We just kept going back and forth until the school bell rang for us to go back into class. It was tied 14/14 when the bell rang.

We were in huddle at the time, and we knew this was the last play of the game— not just for today, but also until the next school year. Without making any eye contact, he said to me, "Everyone, go long, but get this: We'll throw it to Freddie."

I knew what he meant, and what they thought, but I didn't care. I was the target for that throw, and there was no way in hell I was going to look bad. Turns out, he did in fact throw it to me, and I caught it for the touchdown, winning the game. I thought for sure this would get me picked 2nd or 3rd the next time we played, and that motivated me to "train" all summer by playing football with a group of younger kids in the church parking lot. When we weren't playing, I'd jog around town hoping to gain speed so that I could get there first one day, be a captain, and pick a winning team when school started again.

I trained all summer, waiting for that big day—the day school started again, and the football teams were chosen. I waited in the lineup, sure that I was going to get picked early on; after all, I proved myself that last day of school on our recess gridiron. I waited as the captains looked over every kid. I watched them pick the strong guy, the fast guy, the good guy. I realized that everybody seemed to have forgotten my Heisman-worthy play that closed out that game last year.

My heart fell as I watched them pick the all the good kids, then all the okay kids, and then finally the awful kids. I watched them pick the fat guy, the slow guy, and the guy with asthma. I watched, my heart sinking, as the captain came to me. With a look of distaste, he pointed to me, and we all began to run to our makeshift field. I was dead last.

After a while, I passed through the edge where the rotting field was, and I got into the town proper. Same thing, you know, but it's different—shops closed down, or where they're not supposed to be. Some franchising had happened while I was gone; there was a Starbucks now where that old cafe used to be when I was a kid. It was different now, all painted on with that green and white, where I remembered the soft brown and muted tones that used to dot the storefront while I waited for the bus.

It was new for me, that whole school bus experience. In middle school, we switched to a different bus that stopped there, so every morning the middle school kids would stop and wait at the cafe for the new bus to come. Some people would buy soda or rolls to pass the time before our ride. There was an aspiring bully named Robbie that was in the group of travelers. On my first day of 6th grade, he told me horror stories of things he'd do to me once we got to the school. This was solid entertainment to him, sitting at the table that morning, enjoying his coke. Finally, the bus pulled up and everyone started to board. I'd never been on a school bus before, other than taking them to field trips in grade school. Teachers would always accompany us on those trips, though, stopping the anarchy that only middle school boys can start.

As I stepped up into the bus, I started looking for somewhere to sit. I should have just sat in those empty 2 front rows, with the kid with glasses and pimples. It seemed, though, that the "cool" seats were toward the back, where the bus driver couldn't keep a good eye on our activities. I made it all the way to the back of the bus to find not even a single open seat. I turned around and doubled back to the second row on the same side of the driver. About halfway through my first ride on my very first day at a new school, Robbie did something he did not warn me about. It seemed he took a few sugar packets from the café that morning, and he proceeded to rip them open and throw them at my head. The genius thinking behind this was the physics. When the packets hit my head the sudden motion stop caused the contents of the packet to spill in my hair. I tried to get it all out, but the more I ran my fingers though my hair the more it spread. I "enjoyed" my first day in middle school, looking like I had bad dandruff. I suppose I could have had quite a different experience in that school if circumstances were different that first day; things might have been much, much different if I had found a "cool" seat and didn't have to fluff sugar out of my hair.

That wasn't the end of those bus adventures, though, not by a long shot. Sometime in the middle of my sophomore year, I had decided it was time to take some chances and try my hand at starting up conversations with the ladies. On the way home from school one day, I pulled my thoughts together and moved to that vacant 6th seat on the left-hand side, where my classmate Stacy was sitting. I had scoped out the seat, making sure it was empty. I got over there, ready to put my moves on her, all confident with my 6th grade bravado. I made eye contact with her and was trying to think of some cool line, something I could say first. She beat me to it.

"The pimples on your face remind me of my cat's nipples," she said. I was floored. Never in my wildest nightmare would a girl open with a line quite as bold as that. I had no idea how to reply, or even how to spin it in my favor. She had insulted me and brought up nipples all in the same sentence. I sat there, stunned and desperate. I attempted to salvage the conversation any way I could.

"Um...how many cats do you have?" I asked, stammering the words out in an attempt to have some normal conversation.

I don't remember any more of the conversation other than that—at least, not in detail. I remember the feelings I felt, though. I remember that embarrassment and shame when she called me out on my pimples, and the desperate, nervous fumbling for words after she dropped that bomb on me. I remember trying to keep up a normal conversation, numb with shame and anger from her opening salvo. I remember getting off the bus that day, sad that my attempt at being kind and smooth to a girl was met with a cool, calculating destruction of my self-esteem.

Come to think of it, that's the only conversation I can recall with her through all of high school. From that point on, I could barely look at her; her cool gaze reminded me of her words, judging my acne-pocked face and comparing them to her feline nipples. I would walk by her in the hallway, and as I passed her, I could feel the shame behind that one moment on the bus.

Needless to say, I kept to myself for the next year, and I did not initiate any conversations with the ladies. Every time I even thought about it, the pain and shame was fresh in my memory, welling up as if it happened just yesterday. That first attempt on the bus was my last.

I almost did a double take when I passed the gas station, just past the center of town. Of all the things that didn't match my memory, the gas station changed the most. Where there had once been a small gas station was now barely a building at all. The pumps had been torn out of the ground, leaving gaping cracks in the pavement that the grass had reclaimed for its own. The attached mini-mart had all but fallen in on itself; the broken windows allowed me a brief peek inside, to see a crumbling interior and a loft ready to collapse.

It surprised me that the gas station was done and gone; it had been a thriving center when I was a kid. The thing to do on the weekends in this small town was to hang out at one of two places on the weekends: either the gas station or outside the pizza place. Most of the time, we did what teenagers do: we cruised and walked between those two spots, always on the hunt for alcohol and some girls. Often, we hoped those two would come hand in hand.

I can remember one particular night; I was walking from the pizza place to the gas station with a couple of friends. The night had been pretty slow, and we decided, instead of our normal booze-and-babe hunting, we'd go over to the gas station and play some arcade games. The gas station had a little loft up top, away from the main store, where they had a few of the newest games. You could usually find a few guys hanging out there on the weekend. The lure of the buttons was enough to overcome their hunt as well.

As we walked up to the gas station door, I noticed what appeared to be a water-gun fight. Right when I walked up to the door, I felt a stream hit me, and I thought I had gotten caught in some crossfire. That's when I realized that it wasn't so much a water-gun fight as it was my classmate Lonnie shooting directly at my mouth.

It also didn't take long for me to realize the gun wasn't filled with water.

I'd never tasted urine before, but it's pretty much how you would expect it to taste—I guess. It's warmer than you'd think, but that doesn't change the fact that now you're that sorry kid who's tasted some other person's urine. There was much more I should have done; instead, I took it, letting them run away screaming in laughter as I fumbled frantically, gulping and spitting at the water fountain while I fumbled in my pockets for some change to buy a pack of gum.

I still played Pac-Man that night—after the incident. I played until the mini-mart closed, my thumbs mashing out the anger and shame. The gum was a fresh, painful reminder of the reason I was chewing it. Anger and shame, it seemed, were close friends of mine by that point; they had joined up with me sometime when I was younger, and by 11th grade, they knew me pretty well. Even they hung around, laughing and mocking me as I tried to concentrate doggedly on chasing those little ghosts endlessly around the screen.

It was a quick ride, from the field to the hotel; all those memories made it seem longer, though. Memory is a funny thing—time makes no difference there. You could live a lifetime in a second, or a second in an hour. In my particular case, I lived out my childhood in the five minutes it took me to get from that weathered old welcome sign to the hotel where I had made my reservations. The hotel hadn't changed too much, besides "Free Wifi!" signs plastered everywhere. The little living room still had the same furniture I remembered, slightly lighter from years of use; and some of the chairs had been reupholstered, their vibrant new fabric contrasting sharply with their more faded brethren.

I walked over to the counter where the receptionist sat, clacking away at the computer and chatting on her phone. She looked vaguely familiar, but I couldn't place her. She had to have been someone's daughter, since she was too young to have been in school with me. Much to her irritation, I interrupted her to check in.

"Room 12—upstairs to your left. The signing is in the conference room to your right," she said, curtly nodding her head in the conference room's direction.

"Signing for what?" I asked, but she was already nattering away on the phone again. Slightly annoyed, but more curious, I walked the twenty steps or so to the room to see what was going on.

Turns out it was Rocky, that football captain I had reminisced about on my drive over. I guess he was doing some sort of promotion for a local company, since they had these football-shaped pens that they were handing out—you know, the kind that nobody ever really writes with. He was using the pens to sign business cards with the company's name on it and handing it out to whoever asked. I got in line, figuring I might as well say "hi" to the guy after all these years.

I went about 3 or 4 spaces when he suddenly looked up from the signing; he grinned at me, and I grinned back, waving slightly. He grabbed one of the football pens from the rack and looked back over at me, nodding once. I understood; he got up and threw the football pen at me. It arced across the room in a beautiful spiral, landing neatly in my hands as I stretched them out to receive it. His grin got even wider, and he flashed me a quick thumbs-up. Some people in the room started clapping, others laughed; one old guy yelled, "TOUCHDOWN!"

They settled down and got back into the line, but I didn't. He said everything he needed there, and I did too. I walked out of the conference room and up the stairs to my room. I half-smiled on the walk back up to my room, sticking the football pen in my pocket. In some ways, it was the most real connection with anybody I ever had there, and we never even said a word. After taking a shower, I headed over to the bar that I worked at in my college years. I sat down, and lo and behold, Lonnie was staring at me on the other side.

"What can I get for you?" he asked.

"Well, Lon," I smiled, "so long as you keep your pants zipped up, then how about a scotch neat?"

I expected him to think a bit, and laugh, or apologize, or do something; I expected him to acknowledge that urine-filled water gun from so long ago. He didn't, though; he simply shrugged oddly, pouring the scotch into a highball for me and sliding it my way.

"So, you just passing through..." he said, "out-of-towner?"

"No, Lonnie," I said, "it's me, Freddie."

"Oh shit, Fred!" he said, laughing. "How've you been? I ain't seen you in years, not since we used to hang around at the gas station. What's up with you?"

We started to chat about the times, and where we used to sit, and what we're doing now; but he never, not once, touched on the important stuff—the stuff I remembered. I left the bar feeling—something—I don't know. Something hadn't bridged a gap. I felt like we were two ships, or planes, that kind of passed each other dimly in the night, vaguely and mechanically hailing each other to avoid a cataclysmic crash.

The next morning, I headed over to the diner that was connected to the hotel for a cup of coffee. I sat down at a stool, trying to flag the attention of the waiter. It was Robbie.

"Hey, Robbie." I said. "Can I get a coffee?"

"Hey, Fred! How you been?" he said, coming up over to me. "Of course, you can."

He went back over to the coffee machine, pouring out a mug for me. He plopped it down in front of me.

"Want any sugar with that?" he asked me, shuffling a few sugar packets in his fingers.

"Sure do," I said. I grinned. "But hand 'em over sealed and slow, and keep your hands where I can see them."

He laughed, but not for real—that kind of laugh that people do to be polite, that short, fake laugh—a pity laugh, you know? He slid the sugar packets down the counter, nice and easy, like I had asked him to, and we talked for a while over coffee.

I left the diner the same way I left the bar; hell, it didn't even feel any different. From one machine to the next, just spouting out all the things you're supposed to say in the script.

On my way to the hotel, I stopped in the convenience store to get a paper, a couple of lottery tickets, and another coffee. An old school mate was there too, but she didn't seem to remember me.

"How many cats do you have?" I asked her.

"How did you know I have cats?" Stacy asked.

"Your shirt says I heart cats, so I just assumed," I chuckled.

"Oh, yeah, I love my cats. I'm so glad you asked about them!" she said, all excited. I smiled politely, and I turned to fill out my lottery ticket.

"Got a pen?" I asked the cashier.

"Nope," he said. "Only one I got ran out just a second ago."

"Nevermind—I might have one," I said, rifling through my pockets. I found that football pen in my front one, and I laughed silently to myself. It was the first time I was ever going to write with a football pen. It was fat and awkward, with a big number 12 emblazoned on the middle of it.

"I got one, thanks," I said. That big 12 stared up at me as I put pen to paper, and I marked 12 as my first number. Why the hell not?

"...and you know Snowball recently had a litter? They're adorable and furry..."

I hadn't even realized the woman was still talking. I said something noncommittal, still focused on the paper. I usually do just a quick pick. For some reason, though, I figured I'd put a little more thought into it; that 12 seemed significant, and I figured I'd keep going with some meaningful numbers.

"...got a WONDERFUL offer for the littlest white one of them from..."

I was there for my 20th reunion. I marked down 20 for the next spot; might as well stick with the theme, 12 being a number from my past and all.

"...TERRIBLE dandruff. I had to buy a special shampoo for her. She was dotting the floor with fur..."

My mind flashed back fast to all that sugar falling out of my hair; it was almost automatic when I heard the word dandruff, now. I jotted down 6, for that year.

"...ALMOST went out with him! I can't imagine ever being with a man who did that to cats..."

I irritably tried to ignore her, only putting out terse replies every other sentence. She wouldn't shut up about her damn cats. She sure had become more talkative since 10th grade, I thought. I marked down 10 on the paper.

"...such an AWFUL problem with urine! He'd just start to lick it anywhere he found it. It was disgusting..."

Yeah, it is disgusting. At least he had a choice as to whether he wanted to lick urine or not, I thought bitterly. I remembered the super soaker suddenly, and the gas station, and that night of Pac-Man.

I marked down 11.

"... and all five I gave to Dina! Can you believe it?"

I couldn't take it anymore. My careful number choices were being pounded over by this idiot lady going on and on about her cats and how special they were. I wrote down 5 hastily on the paper, not even thinking, and I gave a polite good-bye, telling her I had to go to the general store. Turns out, she really did love her damn cats.

I spent a whole fifteen minutes trying to get out of there. I was really polite. "Yes...no...of course I remember those bus rides... of course, I think teal is a perfect color for Fluffy's little cat boots..." I wondered briefly if she could see the acne scars. I wondered, in a strange moment of cognizance, if pimple scars look a little like pimples, and if pimple scars still reminded her of her cat's nipples.

When I finally managed to get away, I was mentally exhausted and decided to go back to the hotel and watch HBO. A couple hours later, I turned on the news and stayed up unusually late to watch Letterman. To this day, it irritates me that he didn't get the Tonight Show gig.

I woke up in the morning feeling refreshed and amazing; something about that last night had been cathartic, eye-opening. I was looking forward to the reunion that night, and as I dressed in the morning, I had this feeling of euphoria and elation that I hadn't felt in a long time—a very, very long time. Some days you just get that feeling, you know? For me, it was rare; I relished it though, when it did happen. I was on cloud nine all day. Even when I drove into the city to do some errands, I wasn't frustrated or upset at all; even though it took me a couple of hours to get all the stuff done I needed to, I felt even better at the end of the day than I did when I woke up.

I was a little sweaty from my errands, so I came back to the hotel to freshen up. The evening had begun to creep up as I jumped in the shower, and by the time I finished getting ready, dusk had fallen pleasantly on the city. I felt giddy, almost high; I hummed to myself as I ironed my shirt and combed my hair. I was very much expecting to enjoy that high school reunion. I even put a little extra special preparation into my regular routine—which made me a little late.

I arrived at the reunion about twenty minutes after it started. I didn't chit-chat too much; I had a very specific plan in mind as to who I wanted to see—and when. I had known for quite some time that I was going to make sure that tonight was a night that everyone would not soon forget.

My first target was Rocky. I saw him at the table with the rest of the football guys from high school, chatting and talking about all their old glories and victories. Like the day before, he looked up at me and smiled, waving. I pulled a little thing from my pocket, and I fired it from my arm.

The football pen arced gracefully, in a beautiful spiral, before landing neatly into Rocky's outstretched hand. He caught it and noticed the cashier's check taped to it; I watched him open it, read the memo "Lucky #12", and he looked up at me, open-mouthed. I winked, and kept walking.

I walked over to the bar where Robbie was standing. He didn't notice me, not at first; he was busy talking to some girl I hadn't seen since we graduated.

"Hey," I said to the bartender softly. "Can I get a sugar packet?"

"Just a sugar packet?" he said, confused.

"Yeah."

He shrugged, and handed me the sugar packet. I ripped it open, spilling its contents into the trash bin next to me. I took out another cashier's check from my pocket, folding it up very small and just barely fitting it into the now empty sugar packet; I tossed it at Robbie's head from a distance. He felt the impact on his head, and brushed his hand through his hair, grabbing the packet. He pulled the check out and looked at it, gaping. It said: "You gave me some sugar in 6th grade. I'm just returning the favor."

I didn't stop to see the rest of his reaction; I had to do this fast. I moved over to Stacy, sitting down next to her. I leaned over and palmed the check into her hand, and whispered, "I hope you were wrong about the nipples. I'd hate for any poor cat to look like that on any side. Thanks for that 10th grade ride, and I hope Dina's five cats do okay."

She looked at me, confused, as I walked away; I saw that same awed, paralyzed shock on her face as the last. One more to go...

I walked up to Lonnie, the same way I did to Stacy, and I simply palmed him the check and whispered, "I broke everybody's high score in Pac-Man that night in 11th grade."

There was already a buzz about me going on; I could hear it. I bee lined for the door and made my exit. There was no reason for me to stay, not anymore; I had re-connected, re-grounded myself, and now it was time for me to leave. And if a few people were a million dollars richer.

Well, like I said, they deserved it.

SEND ME AN EMAIL

Thank you for reading my book! Please email me at eddielance42@gmail.com. I would love to hear from you and get feedback about my stories and recipes.

You can also ask for me to send you a PDF of just the recipes all together.

As a self-published author, I would really appreciate reviews if you enjoyed my book. Please leave your honest review on Amazon. It will take a few moments and will help me out so much.

www.ingramcontent.com/pod-product-compliance
Lightning Source LLC
Chambersburg PA
CBHW071357290426
44108CB00014B/1585